THE YOUTH WORKER
BOOK OF HOPE

TIM BAKER

ZONDERVAN®

ZONDERVAN.com/
AUTHORTRACKER
follow your favorite authors

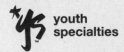

youth
specialties

YOUTH SPECIALTIES

The Youth Worker Book of Hope
Copyright 2009 by Tim Baker

Youth Specialties resources, 300 S. Pierce St., El Cajon, CA 92020 are published by Zondervan, 5300 Patterson Ave. SE, Grand Rapids, MI 49530.

ISBN 978-0-310-28364-5

Cover design by Toolbox Studios
Interior design by Brandi Etheredge Design

Printed in the United States of America

09 10 11 12 13 14 • 20 19 18 17 16 15 14 13 12 11 10 9 8 7 6 5 4 3 2 1

This book is dedicated to you, the hard-working, stay-up-late-counseling, putting-your-life-on-hold youth worker. It's our hope that the stories on these pages will help in those times when you feel as if your life and ministry are falling apart.

Acknowledgments

Thanks to the Youth Specialties publishing team for their dedication and hard work on this project. You people are fantastic.

Thanks to Doug Davidson for devoting your expert editing skill to this book. This book is proof of the amazing work you do.

Thanks to the authors who worked hard to write insightful chapters for this project. You did an incredible job sharing your stories, and putting up with the process of reviewing and revising your work. Thanks for contributing your skill, wisdom, and experience to this project.

Thanks to my wife, Jacqui, and my kids, Nicole, Jessica, and Jacob, for giving me time to work on this project. I love you!

—Tim Baker

CONTENTS

INTRODUCTION
By Tim Baker

MY FIRST YOUTH MINISTRY POSITION WAS IN A CHURCH near Daytona Beach, Florida. You could see the beach from the front door of the church. It was their first shot at a summer youth ministry intern, and it was my first time in the ministry. I remember feeling like it was a gamble for both of us. It was humbling to try to start a ministry together with the associate pastor, who was incredibly skilled at both managing and leading youth ministry.

My laid-back attitude didn't work well in seminary, but it totally worked in student ministry. My inability to learn biblical Greek was embarrassing back at school, but the students who attended our ministry didn't care about that. They wanted a listener and a beach bum. Biblical translation skills weren't at the top of their list.

I got discouraged—quickly. After about half a summer, there was a lot of beach happening, but not a lot of transformation—at least not transformation I could see. I naively expected after a few good youth talks there'd be some kind of mass religious experience, as if someone in our youth group had found the face of Jesus on a piece of toast. Instead I got a tepid response. Students weren't asking the wrong questions; they weren't asking *any* questions. They were engaged when we surfed, but their eyes glazed over any time I opened a Bible. They didn't care too much about painting the house of a mentally challenged lady, but they loved game nights.

I'm not here to play around, I thought to myself. But that's what they wanted—an adult who was willing to put his religion away for a bit and just be human. I struggled. I was frustrated they didn't get it. What was wrong with these kids?

One day, in the midst of all this, the senior pastor walked into a meeting the associate pastor and I were having. Really it was just small talk about upcoming events, camp plans, and our trips to the beach. He listened for a minute and then, as he was about to leave, offered one of the most important ministry truths I've ever learned. On his way out the door, as the associate pastor and I continued discussing all the stuff we had on the Big Youth Ministry Calendar, the senior pastor said, "We'll know in about 15 years if this stuff really worked."

I've remembered that comment ever since. I think that guy was completely right. It's not always 15 years. Sometimes it's five. Sometimes it's just a month. But the point he was making was this: Youth ministry is an investment—and one in which we don't always get to see immediate results.

> YOUTH MINISTRY IS AN INVESTMENT— AND ONE IN WHICH WE DON'T ALWAYS GET TO SEE IMMEDIATE RESULTS.

God has called us into this ministry because of who we are, who he's created us to be. We jump in with passion and a Bible, and we give our lives. And we keep giving our lives until God calls us in another direction, into another ministry. Sometimes we get to see an immediate response—a student comes to the altar after we speak or talks with us in the church van at the end of an outreach event. Sometimes we find out many years later that a seed we planted in a student's life took root. Sometimes we never know what kind of difference we might have made.

If you're in student ministry, you already know that some of the stuff that happens as we invest in the lives of kids is great. Memories are created. Relationships are forged over water-balloon wars and shaving-cream fights and all-night events. We learn very quickly God's call into youth ministry isn't what some people would consider a "real" job. While our friends are moving up the corporate ladder, we're trying to decide how many finger blasters we need. While they're preparing for corporate meetings, we're hanging out in school lunchrooms. We do so because we understand eternal investments are forged one sandwich at a time, one conversation at a time—one student at a time.

These kinds of investments drain us. Not all the stuff that happens in our lives while we're investing qualifies as super, great, or even healthy. Sometimes the stuff that happens to us as we work with students can be painful, damaging, and discouraging. Parents tear us apart. Pastors trample over us. Volunteers challenge our leadership. Students break our hearts. Events cave in. Sometimes it just takes one awkward moment for our self-worth to drop lower than low and, suddenly, we're undone. Those moments can create a cloud of hopelessness that eats into our hearts and sabotages the investment we're making.

And it's in those moments—the times when hope feels more foreign than a new tongue—we need someone who has been where we are, in that hopeless place, to reach in and pull us up.

You know, we toss around a lot of words in student ministry. Words like *core group, commitment, budget, attendance, leadership,* and *outreach* can sometimes feel as if they end up driving our ministry. We wake up every morning letting our to-do list push our day forward until we're tired beyond tired. We feel the senior pastor's breath on the backs of our necks; we know parents are watching. In the midst of all this, hope becomes a forgotten word. It's lost in our prayer time. It's submerged in our board reports. It's buried under the paper on our desks.

I don't know if you've ever been in the place where you and hope are complete strangers. If you've ever been there, take a moment to reflect on those times. What killed your hope? What stole the joy out of student ministry? A parent? A pastoral relationship? A failed event? Another youth worker?

Or was it you?

I've been a part of enough hopeless ministry moments to know I'm usually the first person I blame when things go wrong and the first person I take my frustrations out on. One rotten moment in ministry and I begin to take myself apart. I could have been smarter. I should have worked harder. I "woulda, coulda, shoulda" myself until I'm completely empty. In those moments I fail to remember that ministry isn't about me and what I do. I lose track of Scriptures like:

...the Spirit helps us in our weakness. We do not know what we ought to pray for, but the Spirit himself intercedes for us with groans that words cannot express. And he who searches our hearts knows the mind of the Spirit, because the Spirit intercedes for the saints in accordance with God's will. (Romans 8:26-27, NIV)

How come we so often forget that, in those times we feel so hopeless we don't know what to say to God, he says it for us? That's a passage we need in that moment, yet it's one we often forget. But that's not the only one. Here's another:

Consider it pure joy, my brothers and sisters, whenever you face trials of many kinds, because you know that the testing of your faith produce perseverance. Let perseverance finish its work so that you may be mature and complete, not lacking anything. (James 1:2-4)

Joy and *perseverance* are two words I don't really want to hear when I'm going through the toughest times, but James reminds us they're an essential part of the struggle. Why does God want us to face our trials with joy and perseverance? I'm not sure I fully understand it—but if they're part of God's process of helping us become "mature and complete," I think it's worth it. And here's one more passage:

Do not be anxious about anything, but in every situation, by prayer and petition, with thanksgiving, present your requests to God. And the peace of God, which transcends all understanding, will guard your hearts and your minds in Christ Jesus. Finally, brothers and sisters, whatever is true, whatever is noble, whatever is right, whatever is pure, whatever is lovely, whatever is admirable— if anything is excellent or praiseworthy—think about such things. Whatever you have learned or received or heard from me, or seen in me—put it into practice. And the God of peace will be with you. (Philippians 4:6-9)

Maybe this is the promise we need most when we're feeling hopeless. This is God saying, "Calm down. I give you peace. Rest in that." Which is, of course, often difficult to remember and live out, and yet it's what we need when we're hopeless. Those verses get us going again in the ministry. They remind us about our connectedness to something way bigger than our local student ministry.

We need hope in our ministries. We crave it. But in those days when we're worn down, those times when it feels like all the hard work offers so little reward, rediscovering hope feels nearly impossible. I know. That same summer when most of the kids didn't seem to care about Scripture was also the first time I was confronted about sin, the first time I learned (the hard way) about incorrect information on a flier, the first time I got yelled at by a parent, and a host of other hope-threatening experiences. Every day in our ministries we're challenged to rediscover hope. But how can we do that? How do we build our hope?

> WE NEED HOPE IN OUR MINISTRIES. WE CRAVE IT. BUT IN THOSE DAYS WHEN WE'RE WORN DOWN, THOSE TIMES WHEN IT FEELS LIKE ALL THE HARD WORK OFFERS SO LITTLE REWARD, REDISCOVERING HOPE FEELS NEARLY IMPOSSIBLE.

WE BUILD HOPE BY FOCUSING ON WHAT MATTERS MOST.

Ever met someone who has been so hurt by a ministry situation that it's all they talk about? You ask another youth pastor if she knows a good pizza place, and she goes off on a diatribe about how Mrs. So-and-So blasted her for the kind of pizza she brought to the lock-in six months ago. Or you start chatting with some guy at a ministry convention, and within two minutes he's turned the conversation to his mean-spirited counseling pastor. Our hurts can cause us to focus only on ourselves—and when we do that, we lose hope.

Writing from a prison cell, the apostle Paul has some thoughts that might offer some perspective to those of us who love to make our problems the focus of our ministry. Remember his words? They go something like—

Now I want you to know, brothers and sisters, that what has happened to me has actually served to advance the gospel. As a result, it has become clear throughout the whole palace guard and to everyone else that I am in chains for Christ. And because of my chains, most of the brothers and sisters have become confident in the Lord and dare all the more to proclaim the gospel without fear. (Philippians 1:12-14)

Paul could have written, "Look, people, prison is the worst. Pray for me, because life here is miserable." But he didn't. His eyes weren't focused on his physical chains. Instead, Paul saw the spiritual chains of the guards who kept watch over him. And by keeping his eyes focused on the things that matter most, Paul offered a life-changing hope that affected those guards for eternity. We don't hope because we know we'll survive. We hope because our hope does something in the lives of others. Even when we're at our lowest, hope still changes students.

WE BUILD HOPE BY RETURNING TO THE WELL.
I love the story of Jesus talking with the woman at the well in John's gospel. Even if you've not returned to that Scripture recently, I bet you remember the highlights. Sin and salvation meet over a drink of water, and ultimately the power of salvation is more powerful than sin. The result is new life—not just for this Samaritan woman, but also for many others who heard her story. This woman's passionate story, the story built on the hope of new life, changed people's lives—then and now.

In student ministry, I think we often reduce *hope* to *survival*. When we get through a weekend event and finally get to rest, when we exit a parents' meeting without bruises, we have *survived*, and the relief brings hope. But hope shouldn't be built on something so temporary. Hope is built on returning to the well where we encounter Jesus, letting him remind us why we're living in the first place, and then allowing the living water he provides to spill into the lives of the students we love. Hope built on human survival is empty and hollow. Hope connected to the living and life-changing presence of Jesus builds contagious hope in our student ministry.

WE BUILD HOPE BY REMEMBERING WHO'S IN OUR CORNER.

When we forget God is cheering us forward, despite our mistakes, the things we do wrong become the meat of our ministry. We live an embarrassed identity. When we think of our ministry, we think only of our foul-ups.

But think about Moses. He's one of the kings of all leadership mistakes. He made quite a few bad moves—everything from trying to avoid God's call because he was a lousy speaker to striking the rock at Meribah to allowing Miriam and Aaron plenty of opportunities to spread their own frustration about him. But like Moses, we can take hope because it's not about our mistakes.

> THE POWER OF OUR MINISTRY IS "GOD IN OUR CORNER." THAT'S THE SOURCE OF THE POWER AND THE REASON FOR HOPE.

It's not even about learning from our mistakes, though I think God loves it when we're able to do that. The power of our ministry is "God in our corner." That's the source of the power and the reason for hope. Can you hear God in the corner of your youth room trying to shout louder than the music or the voices of your students? I believe God is there, watching and cheering the entire time we're trying to share the truth of his love with our students.

We all go through moments of extreme weakness, and in those moments our hope can fade. We live through deep personal struggles, and those moments challenge our faith. We experience the worst of the worst in our ministry, and sometimes those dark days coincide with lowest moments in our personal lives. Those difficult moments drain us of the God-focus at the times when we most need it.

If you're in that place right now, whatever the reason may be, we hope this book will be that open hand in your darkness. *The Youth Worker Book of Hope* is filled with stories from people who are in the trenches for God, seeking to be his light in the lives of students he loves. These youth workers know they don't have student ministry all figured out. Each of them has journeyed to that place where hope is hard to find—whether it's due to a failed youth event, an angry parent, a big mistake, a struggling student, or some other challenge. And each of them has lived through that time of trial to talk about how it felt and how they found God's hope.

You may know a few of the people in this book. Maybe you've heard one or two of them speak, or you've read something they've written. But these youth workers aren't sharing their stories in hopes you'll invite them to speak to your staff or buy their newest books. We'd like this book to be a praise offering to God, an offering of thanks for those moments when he's met us and built up hope in us. And we'd be thrilled if, through hearing our stories, you're helped along in your own youth ministry journey.

Investing in kids is tough work. None of us should ever try to go it alone.

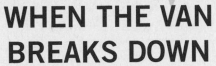

CHAPTER 1

WHEN THE VAN BREAKS DOWN
By Dave Ambrose

I WAS HEADED OFF FOR A WEEK OF SUMMER CAMP WITH A handful of students from our ministry—and this year I'd convinced Adam to come with us. Our church had been very intentional about reaching out to kids in our community who had no religious or spiritual background, and Adam completely fit the bill. I'm pretty sure the only reason he came to youth group in the first place was because our family-life center had an indoor gym, and Adam loved to hoop it up. But somewhere along the way Adam had become more and more interested in what was going on at youth group. And with support from a few volunteer youth workers who played ball with him every week, he'd also grown interested in what God was doing in his life. So when I asked Adam if he wanted to come to camp with us and play basketball all week, his only question was: "Where do I sign up?"

Now of course I've heard many friends in ministry tell horror stories about how they'd been stranded and left for dead on more than one occasion when the church van broke down. But our church had just purchased two brand-new 15-passenger vans. All I had to do was decide which one we'd take to camp.

As the day we were leaving approached, guess whose job it was to make sure the van was filled with gas and ready to go? You got it—yours truly. I remember stepping into the garage where the two new vans were parked and deciding we'd take the blue one. I hopped in the van to take it over to the gas station and fill it up so we'd be ready to go. Wow! I'd experienced the new-car smell before, but the new-van smell took things to a completely different level! It was incredible.

And the van had all the newest features, including a CD player with surround-sound speakers! (That was really something back in the day. Most church vans didn't even have a radio.) This was going to be a trip of a lifetime. What luxury. What ingenuity. I could hardly wait! After filling it with gas, I drove the van back to the church and tucked her snug as a bug back into the garage where she would wait for just a couple more days.

Finally the day arrived for us to leave for camp. I got to the church early, grabbed the keys to the blue van, and headed down to the garage to pull her out and get her warmed up. As I opened the garage door, I couldn't believe what I saw. The blue van was gone! I stood there for a minute trying to compose myself. Then I ran back into the church building, flung open the door to the office, and grabbed the sign-out log for the vans. I looked up our dates and, sure enough, I'd forgotten to sign out the blue van for our trip! That van was already several hundred miles north, carrying our senior citizens' group on their trip to the Land of Eternal Christmas or something like that.

My heart skipped a beat as I turned the page to see if the gray van was available. Thankfully it was. I quickly scribbled my name on the appropriate line and even backdated it so it would look like I'd reserved it weeks earlier. (I have no idea why I felt I had to do that.) Then I grabbed the keys and ran back down to the garage to pull the gray van around to the front of the church.

As soon as I started the van, I noticed the gas tank was completely empty. But I remember thinking how smart I'd been to get to the church so early. I made sure I still had the church credit card and ran to the gas station for another fill-up. By the time I got back, a few kids were already waiting outside with their parents. You could tell by their body language they were very excited about going to camp!

After the other kids arrived, we loaded our bags and camp gear into the back of the van before gathering for prayer. I remember listening as one of the parents prayed for our safety on the trip, but I had no idea how important that prayer would actually become. We hopped in the van, got everyone situated, and waved our goodbyes as we pulled out of the church parking lot.

For the first little while, everything went smoothly. I couldn't believe how great the trip was going. Kids were talking to each other (between rocking songs in surround sound), and we were all sharing what we were looking forward to most about camp. Adam was sitting in the front passenger seat next to me and was peppering me with questions about what to expect and what camp food tasted like. He had his basketball gear on, held his basketball in his hands, and said he was excited about teaching me the "finer points of the game."

I REMEMBER LISTENING AS ONE OF THE PARENTS PRAYED FOR OUR SAFETY ON THE TRIP, BUT I HAD NO IDEA HOW IMPORTANT THAT PRAYER WOULD ACTUALLY BECOME.

After a few hours the kids agreed to turn the music down a bit because a few of them wanted to grab some shuteye before embarking on a sleepless week of camp. I remember watching Adam doze off in the front passenger seat. He even started snoring. I tried to keep myself awake as we drove down the long, lonesome, two-lane highway leading up to camp. The sun was beginning to set, we were in the middle of nowhere, and the entire world seemed at peace. If we kept making such good time, we'd arrive at camp just in time for dinner.

All of a sudden, completely out of nowhere, something exploded on the front passenger side of the van. I had to use every ounce of energy to keep the van from flipping over into the ditch next to the highway. Everyone jolted awake. The explosion completely freaked out Adam, who woke up in a flash, smashed his hands against the front dashboard, and yelled "holy $#%&!" (Which wasn't very funny at the moment with an entire van full of church kids, but looking back, it still cracks me up.)

Somehow I was able to maintain control of the van and slow it down enough to pull safely over to the side of the highway. We all jumped out to find the front tire on the passenger side had completely blown out. Once I saw the tire I understood why it had been so difficult to control the van at 55 mph, and I was even more thankful none of us was hurt. Darkness was quickly creeping in as we sat by the roadside in the middle of nowhere. I knew I had to get this thing changed fast! I asked the kids to help me unload our luggage so we could get to the spare tire and jack. I was hoping another driver would stop and offer to help, but there was no one on that road except us. (This was before cell phones, so we were really stranded.)

After we got the van completely unloaded, I spent the next few minutes trying to undo the cover on the storage space where the spare tire and jack were kept. It was unbelievable. What? Do you need a PhD to figure this thing out? Thankfully Adam was able to help me get it open so we could grab the spare tire.

But what I saw next made my stomach drop. The spare tire (in the brand new church van, mind you) was completely flat! Now what was I going to do? I was the only adult on the trip, responsible for 10 kids now standing by the side of the road next to our broken-down church van, and I didn't even have a spare tire. Why didn't they offer a class on handling these kinds of situations in Bible college? Greek wasn't going to help me much here.

It was at that moment when Adam (the unchurched kid, remember) looked at the rest of the group and said, "I think we'd better say a prayer. There's no way out of this without the Big Guy's help."

Now I know I was the pastor—and maybe I should've been embarrassed that I wasn't the one who suggested we pray. But Adam's words brought a huge smile to my face, and I turned to him and agreed, "That's a great idea Adam. Why don't you lead us in a word of prayer?"

Adam seemed uncertain. "I've never prayed out loud before."

I looked him right in the eye and responded, "That's all right, man. You just say what comes to your mind, and I know God will hear you."

I'll never forget Adam's prayer. I think it may be the reason we broke down in the first place. It's amazing what God will do to spend some time with us.

"God, we're in some deep $#%& (clearly Adam liked that word), and there's no way out of this unless you send some help," he prayed. "And you better do it quick, because I gotta go to the bathroom, and it's a long walk to camp. Amen."

The entire group broke out laughing and high-fiving Adam, telling him how great his prayer was. It wasn't even five minutes later when we saw a pair of headlights coming down the road toward us. I asked the kids to stay put while I tried to wave this other vehicle down to see if we could get some help. It turned out to be another church van (much older and more beat up than ours, but theirs was still moving) filled with kids on their way to the same camp. After a few minutes of explanation (and a few laughs at my expense), the other youth worker agreed to go ahead to the camp and send back some help for us. I thanked him and we waited until help arrived. The camp sent another van to pick us up and we still got there in time for dinner. We left our brand-new van sitting by the side of the road until the next day, when I was able to go back and take care of it with some help from the camp staff.

I'm happy to say we had a great time at camp that week, and Adam began following Jesus in a completely fresh way.

WRONG TURNS AND MISSED EXITS
Obviously there's nothing you can do to ensure you'll never break down on a long trip with a group of kids. But looking back, it's clear I made a few mistakes:

1. I forgot to sign out the van and do a pre-trip inspection.
Even though I thought I didn't have anything to worry about because our church had two brand-new vans, I shouldn't have taken anything for granted. There's a lot to remember for any trip you take! When you're taking kids along with you, no matter what you're transporting them in, I've found it's a great idea to have a written checklist to review before you even leave home. I was very fortunate our church's other van was still in the garage. What would I have done if I'd arrived that morning and both vans were gone? It would've been a nightmare, and it would've cost me a certain amount of credibility with both kids and parents.

2. I didn't have an emergency plan mapped out.

Another mistake I made was failing to have an emergency plan in place if something were to go wrong. No matter what kind of vehicles you drive, no matter how great your ministry ideas are, there's always a risk of something unexpected happening. If I'd given it a little more thought, I'd have realized I needed another youth leader with me, maybe even following me in a different vehicle in case something like this happened. But I never took the time to think it all through in advance.

WHEN YOU OPEN YOUR MINISTRY AND ACTUALLY INVITE OTHER PEOPLE TO HELP, YOU BUILD A BROADER BASE OF OWNERSHIP. YOU GIVE OTHERS OPPORTUNITIES TO USE THEIR GIFTS TO GLORIFY GOD. AND YOU GET THE CHANCE TO SEE GOD AT WORK THROUGH ALL THE DIFFERENT PARTS OF HIS BODY— THE CHURCH.

3. I tried to do it all myself.

I'm sure you're familiar with the Old Testament story about Moses trying to do everything himself and acting as ultimate judge and jury for the entire Jewish nation. I've taught this story to my own youth groups many times. So why are there still so many times when I try to do it all myself—in my life and in my ministry? Am I too proud to ask for help? Maybe I'm too insecure? Do I think asking someone else to come alongside and share the load is a sign of weakness? It took good ol' Jethro to straighten Moses out and get him started down the right path toward delegation. What's it going to take in my life?

When you do everything yourself, you may feel like things get done a little more quickly. You may think it's the best way to ensure things get done the way you want them done. But you also miss out on quite a bit. When you open your ministry and actually invite other people to help, you build a broader base of ownership. You give others opportunities to use their gifts to glorify God. And you get the chance to see God at work through all the different parts of his body—the church. And that's quite a sight to see!

4. I didn't really trust God would show up.

God is seldom early, but he's never late. Why do I have such a difficult time trusting God with all the intimate details of my life? As we stood by the side of the road next to our broken-down van that day, I honestly had no idea what to do next. I didn't know where to turn. But Adam did. He knew we needed to pray and ask God to help us. He knew this situation was giving us the opportunity to learn to trust God and see what he was going to do. Lord, help that become *my* first instinct as well.

FINDING HOPE

No matter how well you plan things out, you can never assure everything will go smoothly. Bad things happen to every single one of us. As a youth worker you've probably already experienced at least one situation in which you did everything possible to prepare, yet things still went horribly wrong. (If not, don't worry—your time is coming!) We can't control everything, and we can't prevent bad things from occurring in our lives. But I'm a firm believer everything happens for a reason because I believe God is sovereign. He's interested in, and in charge of every detail of our lives, and he wants to be involved—if we'll only invite him to be. God will never force himself on us. We have to ask him to get involved. We have to invite him into every little crease and crevice of our life.

And when we do ask God to get involved, we'll often find that the help God offers comes through the body of Christ—through other Christians seeking to follow God's leading. That's not always easy for us to accept. If I'm really honest with myself, I have to admit that when the other youth pastor and his team came down the road and rescued us, it was difficult for me. When the camp staff helped me work it all out and drove back with me the next day so we could get our van back up and running, it was difficult for me. I was afraid of what people were thinking about me. I was afraid of being tagged as a failure. I was embarrassed I needed to ask for help. I guess I was just feeling insecure about who I was and how capable I was of doing the job I was called to do. The truth is I still am at times. I need to learn to be okay when other people come alongside to help. I need to see these times as opportunities for God to minister to me through others. Instead of kicking back against it, I want to learn to open myself to this and watch God work.

By the way, we got home from camp safe and sound, and the entire experience was an unforgettable adventure! The experience has stuck with me through the years because it taught me a lot about God's protection and his intervention in my life. And it was also a wonderful reminder of the ways God is working in the lives of kids—even kids like Adam who we might think are just along for the ride.

We all seemed to meet God in our own way that day by the side of the highway. I'll never forget the way God showed up as we stood there in the middle of nowhere next to our broken-down van. How are you depending on God to show up in your life and ministry today?

CHAPTER 2

WHEN PARENTS DON'T RESPECT YOU

By Brenda Seefeldt

A DETAILED MINISTRY PLAN IN A THREE-RING BINDER: That's what got me my first youth-ministry job back in 1985.

The church's previous youth pastor had been there more than 10 years, and after a year without a youth pastor, they were ready for something new. I brought my plan to the interview, and let's just say it was detailed: It spelled out everything, right down to the application forms I'd use for each small group. Since I was pretty sure of myself and my plan, I answered their questions with a bit of cockiness. Despite my attitude, I still felt deeply grateful when they hired me. I *really* wanted to be a part of this church.

During the year they'd spent without a youth pastor, a set of parents had been doing all the youth ministry work. They were very capable leaders, and I was excited to have them join my team. But our first conflict came almost immediately when they wouldn't fill out the three-page leadership application I gave them. They just couldn't bring themselves to do it. When they talked to me about their difficulty with the application, I was black-and-white about it. I told them filling out the application was absolutely essential. But after months of their "defiance," I agreed to accept them without the application. And I patted myself on the back for my flexibility.

You see, I had a very clear, predefined vision of what a volunteer youth ministry staff should look like—and parents really weren't a big part of it. I'd overly bought into adolescent development theories about the importance of teens having distance from their parents so they could grow in their faith. These parents had a different view. We butted heads often.

Because they were good parents, good leaders, and good Christians (a view I now have with hindsight), they tried everything possible to work with me. I vaguely remember a lunch meeting in which one mom tried to find a way to get through to me about the value and influence of parents. I remember how uncomfortable the lunch was, and I even recall what table we sat at. But I don't remember at all what she was trying to tell me. I know I wasn't listening. I went to lunch not ready to listen.

> I HAD A VERY CLEAR, PREDEFINED VISION OF WHAT A VOLUNTEER YOUTH MINISTRY STAFF SHOULD LOOK LIKE—AND PARENTS REALLY WEREN'T A BIG PART OF IT.

The final breakdown in my relationship with this mom occurred when her son gave me the "letter" he'd received as a high school athlete before he left for college. He told me he wanted me to have the letter because I'd had a significant role in his life and faith. That meant a lot to me. But his mother asked me to give the letter back. I said no—and our relationship suffered greatly.

I'm sad to say there were many other parents whose respect I lost over the years. I mention this mom in particular because she was one of the parents who tried hardest to help me see correctly. But I just couldn't.

Many years later I read The Barna Group's report *Third Millennium Teens* and had an epiphany. Of all the good insights from this report, this quote rocked me:

Many of the church leaders talk about the importance of the family, but in practice they have written off the family as an agency of spiritual influence. Their assumption is that if the family (including teenagers) is going to be influenced, it is the organized church that will do the influencing, primarily through its events—worship services, classes, special events, etc. This philosophy causes the impetus behind youth ministry to be fixing what is broken—that is, to substitute the efforts of the church for those of parents since most of the latter do not provide the spiritual direction and accountability that their children need. But there is a procedural problem here: kids take their cues from their family, not from their youth ministers. God's plan was for the church to support the family, and for the family to be the front-line of ministry within the home. Teenagers may glean some truths and principles from youth leaders, but the greatest influence in their lives will remain their parents. What are youth ministries doing to serve families rather than usurp them?

That quote, and particularly that final question—*What are youth ministries doing to serve families rather than usurp them?*—echoed in my head for a long time. I knew that, despite my good intentions, I'd usurped the role of many parents over the course of my time in ministry. I'd written my youth ministry plan in 1985 (I still have the dot-matrix printed copy), but it wasn't until 1999 that I read the Barna report. I'd been disrespecting parents for years. I thought I was supposed to be the chief spiritual influencer of the lives of these teens, but I'd usurped their parents' God-given role. I'd made them feel inadequate as parents.

It's no wonder so many parents disrespected me. I'd always been aware of the parents' feeling about me, but I justified it or excused their feelings because there was fruit in their teens' lives. I always thought those parents would eventually come around and see how brilliant I was. (There was that cockiness again.) After all, I was being given high school letters and other gifts that reinforced this thinking.

WHAT I DID WRONG

Since that epiphany I've changed nearly everything about how I lead in youth ministry. As I reflected on the insights from the Barna report and my own experiences with the parents of kids I'd been working with, the mistakes I'd been making became clear:

1. I made parents feel inadequate.

Truth is, parents already feel inadequate without us youth pastors making it worse. There are lots of reasons parents feel inadequate when raising kids. Their own children make them feel that way. Parenting books make them feel that way. TV makes them feel that way. So it is no wonder I, in my great passion and knowledge, made parents feel inadequate, too. I operated from the belief that parents had no real part to play in a youth ministry (unless I needed them to drive, of course). My actions weren't intentional, but the message was clear to parents who already felt inadequate.

2. I didn't want to face the truth that parents could make me feel inadequate.

The parents who tried to work with me were gifted and wise. They understood teens. They openly showed sacrificial love to their children. What a blessing they could have been to other teens. But they made me feel inadequate, even with my three-ringed youth ministry plan. If only they would've filled-out that application, I would've gained some leverage—or so I thought.

I always felt deeply saddened that there were some teens I poured my heart and soul into who just didn't make it. I often acknowledged that those teens who did make it were most often the ones with good parents. Duh. But I never tapped into this influence. I have a lot of parents whose forgiveness I need to seek.

It's important to remember that we, as youth pastors, can't replace the important role parents play in the lives of their kids. But we do have things we can offer to parents—our knowledgeable window into the adolescent world as well as our passion for the faith. Parents want to hear our perspective. They want us to partner with them. And they want our help to ease their own fears of inadequacy and help them share their faith.

3. By ignoring the importance of parents, I was running a "drycleaner" youth ministry.

One common complaint among youth workers is "drycleaner" parents—those who drop their children off at youth group expecting to come back 90 minutes later to find their kids returned to them all clean, proper, and practically sealed in plastic. But that kind of thinking can also infect youth workers. I truly thought I could clean up the youth in my limited time with them. Not only was this a false dream, it encouraged parents to think that way, too.

4. I was leading a Brenda-centric youth ministry.

My humblest realization was that a healthy youth ministry doesn't revolve around me. I assumed I should be at the center of all the action since I was the one hired to do youth ministry. I planned and spoke at all the youth meetings. I planned and attended all the retreats. Relationships with the youth centered on my volunteer staff and me. I often referred to parents as "them" or "the old fogies upstairs." Of course, this was done with good intentions. I was passionate about making a difference in the lives of these kids.

But I was taking on the role of primary spiritual influencer of these youth and using the youth ministry as that agency of influence. Yes, parents could be a part of the volunteer staff (just fill out the application, please). Yes, they could bring food whenever I asked them. But I never asked them to be the spiritual influencers in their own teens' lives.

Guess what happened when I left that church? There was a big vacuum because I'd based the whole youth ministry on me, despite my great written plan. That kind of problem occurs in all too many churches when the youth pastor leaves—but that's another issue for another chapter.

5. I thought parent meetings were all about my agenda.

I've always held parent meetings. They were part of the plan I brought into that first interview. I intended to have a quarterly meeting with parents so they'd be abreast of the youth ministry agenda. How great of me. It never occurred to me that knowing my youth ministry agenda wasn't really helping them be the spiritual influencers of their teens. The parents who came (they were always the good parents) were coming out of desperation, hoping to somehow figure out how the youth ministry could help them raise their beloved flesh and blood. And I was focused on passing out calendars.

I still hold parent meetings, but the format is entirely different now. I find a book, DVD series, or something that encourages parents in their role as chief spiritual influencers. This is the focus of the meetings. (Conveniently, the meetings also give me a chance to distribute calendars.) This is ministry to the parents as well as to the youth.

Here is something that has worked well for me: I introduce a youth-related topic, share a bit from my own perspective as a youth worker, and then invite parents to offer their own thoughts. The meeting always takes on a life of its own as parent after parent share their experiences with the topic and other hurdles they daily face with their teens. Parents encourage one another; parents gain new insight from one another; parents share with one another what they've done or what they've learned the hard way. I always sit back and watch. I haven't told a parent how to parent, but I've provided a safe platform for parents to learn from one another.

FINDING HOPE IN A NEW PERSPECTIVE ON PARENTS
Today I have a very different understanding of the connection between parents and youth ministry. Here are a few of the things I've learned from my experiences:

Parents really are the number one influence on their kids.
If I would dare deflect any of the blame for mistakes I made in relating to parents in my first 18 years of youth ministry, I might blame it on my training. I got my youth ministry education in the 1980s, which is about the same time *youth ministry* became a product. I was taught the importance of the role other significant adults could play in an adolescent's development. I was taught that peers were the most important influence during adolescence. I was shown statistic after statistic (often without the source) of how teens choose the influence of friends over that of parents, teachers, or pastors. I was taught about

the separation stage of adolescence. I was taught a relational style of youth ministry that used the incarnation as example. In my mind, that meant I needed to do all I could to influence vulnerable teens in the short time I was with them. And then there was that heavily-quoted-but-never-credited statistic that 85 percent of Christians came to Christ before their 18th birthday. I had a lot of work to do before it was too late. So what if some of the parents were uncomfortable with the youth ministry?

I have since collected every possible stat on teens and influence with primary and secondary sources. And those statistics all support the same conclusion: Parents are the single greatest influence on teenagers.

As a church ministry (we youth ministers tend to forget we're part of the larger church, not just our own wing—but, again, that's another chapter), we have the responsibility to support the family first and operate in ways that empower parents to be the front line of ministry. Besides, knowing what I know now, why would I usurp this group that has such influence?

I think we make a mistake when we think youth ministry is all about giving teens opportunities to spend time with their peers. Of course time with peers is part of adolescent development. Teenagers will naturally pull away from their parents and begin to model (whether intentionally or unintentionally) new lifestyles and choices of their chosen peer group. But that draw is never stronger than parental influence. Be sure your parents know to never give up!

Through school, after-school sports and clubs, downtime, and weekend time, teens do spend a lot of time with peers. Church doesn't need to be another place where youth are separated from adults, especially when there's the ready-made community of a church family. Kids desire peer-group time, but they also wish for more community. The church family readily provides that.

Parents need to be a primary focus for any healthy youth ministry.
At my current youth ministry, every plan we create, in accordance with our church's vision, involves parents. This isn't the same for ev-

ery church. Perhaps you'll only be able to plan an activity that places parents in a key role once a month or once a quarter. But the bottom line is to find creative ways of providing nonthreatening opportunities that allow parents to share their faith twith their own children. A lot of parents are intimidated by this. Maybe this is due to their colorful past or the immaturity in their own faith, but too many parents doubt they can talk about faith with confidence. Somehow and some way you can be of great help here.

But what about teens whose parents are not part of the church? Very simple. Most of those young people probably came with teens from your church. In most cases these youth know the parents of the friends who brought them and have spent time at their homes. Sometimes these teens even affectionately call their friends' parents "Mom" or "Dad." When parents become part of the youth ministry programming, the youth whose parents are not part of the church fit easily into these families without feeling weird or left out. When parents are supported and released to be that spiritual influence over their own teens, conversations will naturally continue with their teen's friends. Maybe over time you'll build a connection with these other parents, who are no doubt looking for help with raising their children.

This focus also helps with the common problem of visitors to the group feeling left out. In this approach, the outside teen is absorbed into a family unit instead of being the only one who can't find her way into a youth group set of friends.

Our better role is as a master chess player.
I see my ideal role as a youth pastor as if I'm sitting in front of a big chessboard. In this role I'm directing all the pieces of our church to interact with the youth, with the prize being the faith and formation of the teens. I'm not just thinking about my movement or that of the adult volunteer staff and Sunday school teachers. All the people in our congregation—and that includes the widows and the nursery workers, too—are beloved rooks, knights, and queens. My goal is to put them in position to share their faith experiences with our youth. To do this, I use everything the church has to offer, whether it's a

planned event or the weekly bulletin. Everyone and everything is a part of the youth ministry.

At first this description might sound like a return to the Brenda-centered ministry I mentioned earlier. But if I'm really going to work in this way, I can't be at the center of the action. The church family must be the center of everything. My role is to show them the way and equip them to minister to youth.

Adults are generally intimidated by teens for a variety of reasons. But when I see my primary goal as positioning the church family for ministry to its youth, the relationship between the teens and the church family changes. Moving myself out of the center also removes that all-too-easy excuse of "It's the youth pastor's job."

Kara Powell, director of the Fuller Youth Institute, has been advocating for an interesting new ratio between youth and adults in youth ministry. Powell calls for a 5:1 ratio—but that's five *adults* for every single *youth* involved in a healthy student ministry. This doesn't mean finding more volunteer staff. You've got an entire church family ready to be used. You just need to show them how to work with teens and sustain them in their faith.

We must support parents' decisions, even when we disagree.
Gather a group of youth pastors together, and after comparing attendance numbers (yuck), the next topic of conversation is complaints about parents. I don't need those venting times anymore. I've learned to value my parents differently. For example, if a teen is grounded because of grades and a youth group event falls under that grounding, then I understand he is grounded from youth group. I back the parent up in my communication to that teen.

I'm free to do this because I feel peace in my new role. I've given parents everything they need to serve as examples to their kids, to share their faith day in and day out. I compile resources, clues, and ideas and pass them on to parents via email, bulletins, and conversations. I find every possible tool to assist them and pass it on in every possible way. Their children are their responsibility. If they believe their child should be grounded from youth group, I've provided them with plenty of tools to use to help make that grounding a faith lesson. In a sense, they're doing my job. Or, to say it more accurately, I'm now doing the job I should have been doing all along—equipping parents to be the spiritual influencers. I just moved some important chess pieces.

Now that I've made parents central to everything I do in youth ministry, I can honestly say parents respect me now. They may not always understand me. (Sometimes I still may be too passion-driven). They may not always agree with everything I say or do. But communication lines are more open because they know I respect them as parents of the beloved kids who make up the youth ministry.

I've been at my current church for 18 years now, nine of them since my epiphany. That longevity is due solely to my entire church embracing my new role. It helped that the pastoral staff came to this same realization at the same time I did (through a different road) and that we agreed about the shifts that were needed. But the primary changes in the youth ministry were in my attitude and approach. I had to change so parents and the larger church family could become part of the youth ministry.

It didn't take much for the parents to respond when I let them know in every way possible that I supported them and wanted to be a resource to them. Changing my approach toward the parents has meshed my love and passion for teens with the responsibilities of my job perfectly. The workload is very different, but it is also more manageable. And it's also made a promising difference in the lives of our students.

I don't have the words to describe what a blessing longevity has been for me or how blessed I feel to have parents who respect me. But I know that these two go hand-in-hand. I truly believe parents want their church's youth ministry to be a resource to them in helping them raise their own flesh and blood.

By the way, remember that student who gave me his high school letter years ago? Well, he's now 36, and I'm still a faith influencer in his adult life. But I did return the letter to his mom. Although I still get some late-night phone calls from him, I know his parents are the main reason he is such a terrific adult.

CHAPTER 3

WHEN THE FINANCES FAIL

By Will Penner

I GET THE WHOLE MULTIPLYING TALENTS PARABLE IN Matthew 25:14-20, at least to some degree. I mean, if the master gives a talent to his servant and the servant doesn't do anything with it, the master should take it away and give it to someone who will do something with it. I'm also aware of the double entendre of the English word *talent*. I've heard a number of sermons implying that Jesus was talking about how we use our skills and abilities when, in fact, the *talent* was a unit of currency in Jesus' time—a substantial amount of money.

So I understand that if one servant was able to make two talents into four, the master would be pleased. And if another servant turned five talents into ten, the master would be even more pleased—and that's certainly the right person to give the remaining talent to, since that servant has been especially fruitful.

But here's what I want to know: How would the master have reacted if the only talent left when he returned was the one that had been buried? What if the one with two talents invested them both, but it didn't pay off? What if the one with five talents not only didn't have the coins he'd been given, but also had ran up another five talents of debt for the master, because he'd tried really hard, but failed anyway?

I took my first job as a part-time youth minister because I needed some extra cash. (That's why you got into youth ministry, right? For the money?) At the time the only trip my little church youth group had ever taken was a "ski trip" to Gatlinburg, Tennessee. I tried to keep up the tradition that first year, but of the 12 kids who went on the trip, only five were even willing to try skiing the first day (only one kid had skied before)—and only one of those five wanted to return to the slopes a second day. Apparently the annual "ski trip" had become more of a shopping trip.

I guess there's nothing wrong with a shopping trip, even one disguised as a ski trip. But I didn't really think subsidizing such a trip was a good way to use money from the church budget. I don't believe people's tithes and offerings to God should be used to support such ventures. So I decided to do what every other red-blooded American youth minister seemed to be doing: I would take my group on a mission trip.

I looked around a bit for short-term mission agencies that fit my theological and philosophical bent and would help make our kids feel like they were part of something bigger. I was hoping we could offer the kind of experience students would come home excited about.

We settled on a work-camp experience that wasn't too far from home. It was quite affordable and allowed us an opportunity to serve others during the day, then return each evening to an environment where we'd join other youth groups for food, games, activities, and worship. It turned out great, and the seven kids who went had a terrific time.

The following year, 15 participated in the work-camp trip—even though we'd also introduced a foreign mission trip, which kept some students from participating in the domestic one. The number of kids from our church attending this work camp continued to climb steadily each year, as did the participation in some other summer offerings. One summer we had a group of 28 attend—a record year.

The thing about the agency I was working with is that, to get the best prices for a summer experience, we had to pay our deposits before Christmas the previous year. After we took 28 people, I decided to get really bold and book 36 spots for the following year. That was the maximum number allowed to come to a single location from a single church. If our group was any larger, we'd be broken up and sent to different locations.

Given the way the numbers had been growing, a group of 36 felt reasonable. But there were several complicating factors that summer. Our foreign mission trip had taken off, and that year we had 40 people from a few different churches go on the trip we sponsored. We also hosted a mission conference for our area that involved almost all my kids in one way or another. Several students served as junior counselors at our denominational camp. And our church's vacation Bible school relied heavily on youth involvement.

In my mind the work camp was kind of an introductory step into the mission experience, so my "marketing" efforts around it were practically nonexistent. This part of our program seemed to have developed a lot of momentum on its own, so I figured it didn't need much energy from me. So I neglected it—in a big way. In fact, it wasn't until about three weeks prior to our camp date that I realized only five people were registered—and two of those were adult chaperones!

I pleaded with the agency, asking them to allow us to cancel and get back some of the money we'd paid them or just carry the remainder of the deposit over until next year so I could do a better job of encouraging participation. No dice. They rattled off something about it not being fair to other people who had played by the rules, saying they needed to enforce their policies in a way that was "firm, fair, and consistent." That exact phrase was reiterated to me several times—I think it's one of their corporate mantras.

So in one fell swoop, I wiped out almost $10,000 we'd painstakingly saved in dedicated funds over the past four years. Needless to say, some of the parents and other members of the church were quite perturbed to find out I'd wasted nearly $10,000 from their mission fund. I was fortunate to have a very supportive senior pastor whose primary focus was to help me learn from the situation and figure out how to avoid making a similar mistake again. Some of the parents weren't quite as forgiving—in fact, "weeping and gnashing of teeth" comes to mind as I vividly recall their reactions to my faux pas.

But wait—there's more.

Fast-forward a decade. After several years of involvement in various youth ministry publishing efforts, I felt called to start a new magazine devoted to youth ministry. With the blessing of some friends and new partners, I launched a publication called *The Journal of Student Ministries*. The friends and partners involved in the project were terrific. They offered their wisdom, time, and energy—and several of them put their reputations on the line to join forces in this new endeavor. However, other than a family startup loan and a couple of long-term advertising and promotional agreements, I had to fund the enterprise myself.

In essence, my wife and I launched the magazine out of our basement. We were horribly underfunded from the get-go, and frankly, I was in way over my head. And though the publication flourished in many ways, it was a financial flop.

Once we'd extended ourselves beyond anything I could've previously imagined, we sold the publication. (I'm glad to say it's still around; in fact, I now work part-time for the publication I used to own.) But even after the sale, we still remained close to $250,000 in debt! I imagine there are entrepreneurs out there for whom a quarter of a million dollars isn't that big of a hit. But for a youth pastor who moonlighted as a magazine editor, that's a huge amount—and I'm currently working four jobs in order to pay off the debt.

> ONCE THINGS WENT WRONG AND IT APPEARED WE MIGHT LOSE THE FUNDS WE'D PUT UP FOR THE TRIP, I WAS SLOW TO LET OTHERS IN ON THE PROBLEM.

LEARNING FROM MY MISTAKES

Through both of these experiences I've learned a ton. My head and heart are filled with lessons learned as a result of these trying experiences. Let me share just a couple of places where I think things went wrong:

1. I didn't seek enough counsel.

When it came time to decide how many spots we should reserve for the mission trip, I can honestly say it never even dawned on me to ask anyone else's opinion before signing a contract committing the church to those numbers and having our treasurer cut a check for the deposit. When it comes to committing that level of resources, I should've run it by several of the stakeholders—including the senior pastor. I'd have probably made a better decision—or at least I wouldn't have been out there on the limb all by myself.

> IN YOUTH MINISTRY THERE ARE LOTS OF DAY-TO-DAY DECISIONS FOR WHICH WE CAN AND SHOULD RELY ON OUR OWN JUDGMENT. BUT FOR THOSE LARGER, STRATEGIC DECISIONS, WE REALLY NEED TO INVOLVE OTHER PEOPLE. THAT MEANS WE CAN'T LEAVE THOSE DECISIONS UNTIL THE VERY LAST MINUTE.

To make matters worse, once things did go wrong and it appeared we might lose the funds we'd put up for the trip, I was slow to let others in on the problem. I was embarrassed, and I hoped for a while that I'd be able to fix the problem without having to admit my mistake. If I had it to do over again, I'd tell every stakeholder in my ministry what was going on, including my pastor, the elders, the kids' parents, adult volunteers, and any other advocates of the youth ministry. I'd even tell the kids earlier. I'm always pleasantly surprised by students' reactions when I show them my humanness.

Similarly, though I sought some counsel before launching *The Journal of Student Ministries*, when it came to making most of the day-to-day decisions, I made them on my own. Just like in my local church, there were people who would've been happy to be a part of that decision making; I just needed to ask.

2. I hurried the big decisions instead of seeking discernment in community with others.

One of the things I find most frustrating when I sit on church committees is how long it takes to make a decision—especially when I feel like I already know what needs to be done. Sometimes it's like trying to quickly turn a huge boat around, and I have a personality type that just wants to get moving. In those cases, little is more frustrating than trying to build group consensus.

In youth ministry there are lots of day-to-day decisions for which we can and should rely on our own judgment. But for those larger, strategic decisions, we really need to involve other people. That means we can't leave those decisions until the very last minute. Better decisions are often reached after bantering them around in groups, and doing so makes us less likely to find ourselves at the helm of another *Titanic*. I wish I'd relied on a mastermind group of people to make more of the major decisions on the front end of both of those experiences.

3. I held on too long.

Recovery groups say the best definition of *insanity* is "trying the same thing again and again, but expecting different results." Since I'd been making all the decisions and I didn't like the results, you'd think I'd have sought out more guidance and assistance from others—preferably before things spiraled out of control. My holding on too long when things weren't working was particularly apparent in the case of the magazine. My wife was telling me I needed to sell *The Journal* six months and $100,000 earlier than I was willing to make that decision myself. I'm *very* fortunate she doesn't rub my nose in it (not too much, at least).

4. I ignored the laws of physics.

An object in motion tends to stay in motion unless acted upon by another force. When a snowball is gathering momentum, you can bet it'll continue to grow—and become even more destructive—unless something changes its course.

When my children do things they shouldn't and then want to avoid getting into trouble, sometimes lying to me about it seems like a good option at the time. The problem is that the lying usually gets them into even more trouble—and often they have to tell another lie to cover up the first one. Unless someone intervenes, the lies will continue to snowball.

Similarly, when I start making bad decisions, it's as if an unseen force continues to perpetuate more bad decisions. When I try to get myself out of a hole I dug, I often try to use the same shovel that got me into the hole in the first place. God put other people around us for a reason, and sometimes we simply need to get out of the way and let someone else help us get back on course so our negative momentum doesn't keep steamrolling.

HOPE...EVEN WHEN THE MASTER'S TALENTS ARE LOST

When I look at these situations through the lens of Jesus' parable of the talents, I feel I'm the servant who's not even mentioned in the parable—the one who lost *all* the master's talents. Even though a particular church administered the $10,000 youth fund, it was God's money. The same is true with the magazine: We begged, borrowed, and "robbed Peter to pay Paul" for as long as we could. We cashed out our savings, retirement, and kids' college funds. (Yes, I know financial planners like Dave Ramsey and Larry Burkett would be disappointed.) We signed bank notes, accepted loans from family members, and received "unintentional extended credit" from some of our ministry partners. So that was God's money, too—entrusted to us, to me, as its steward. And I blew it.

So I'm the servant who took two talents and *tried* to devote them to something good—a mission opportunity for kids—only to have nothing financial to show for it afterward. And I'm the servant who later took five talents and tried to invest it to create something really good—a kingdom-building resource for youth workers—and not only lost those five talents, but also went another five talents (or more) into debt.

Sometimes those failures cause me to wish I'd followed the lead of the safe, comfortable, one-talent servant who didn't increase his master's holdings. At least he didn't lose it all *and then some*.

On the other hand, Jesus' parable gives me hope. Even though it might *feel* safer not to take a chance, Jesus was crystal clear this was not the steward he was looking for. After all, there's something rather "lukewarm" about being safe. I take comfort in the knowledge that though these experiences certainly don't portray me as someone who was really "hot" and on top of his game in these moments, at least I was really, *really* cold—which Scripture says is better than being lukewarm.

CHAPTER 4

WHEN A STUDENT HATES GOD

By Dave Rahn

YOU KNOW, *HATE* IS SUCH A STRONG WORD. WORKING IN the outreach wing of youth ministry, I've had a few students tell me straight up that this is how they feel about the Lord, life, and all things religious. Misty and Sasha are two students who come to mind who convincingly spit such words out, snarling as they delivered their painful message. Matthew, on the other hand, was eerily calm, sneering as he told me what he thought about God. But their acidic comments hit my spirit with the same burn: *God is a joke. If God thinks I'm just gonna roll with whatever, he's crazy. There's no way I can believe in a God who messes people up like this.* All versions of "I hate God."

Tom was another student in my youth ministry whose anger at God was palpable. Tom had been deeply affected by the death of a close friend. After Dan's death Tom moved into the emotional red zone, looking at me with a hollow, icy stare and declaring he hated God. It took some courage for me to stay centered when Tom dropped that bomb on me.

Dan was a popular, winsome guy who'd served as co-captain of the football team and president of the student body. After Dan came to Christ on a backpacking trip I'd led into the Smokies, he came back ready to change his world. I've honestly never seen anyone so thoroughly grab hold of the fundamental truth that the secret to the Christian life is to fully abandon oneself to Christ. Dan, already a life-of-the-party type of guy, was living *large* for Jesus! It was only a matter of time—and not much time, at that—before Dan would tell his younger next door neighbor, Tom, about the Lord. And it wasn't a fair fight when the senior put the challenge in front of the freshman. Tom wanted what Dan had and began to do his best to follow Dan as Dan followed Christ.

Within a month a terrible tragedy would rock us all. Dan was involved in a freakish accident where he was instantly killed. Troy, another student involved in the accident, survived, but spent months recovering in a burn unit. All of us were in shock, staggering about in disbelief as we tried to make sense of what had happened. I was just a youth ministry rookie, only two months removed from my college graduation—and nothing I'd learned as a Bible major was helping me minister through this crisis.

For a year or so, those of us who'd been closest to Dan shared a quiet bond as we propped one another up in the faith. Though he had been walking with Christ for just four weeks when he died, he'd set a nearly impossible standard to follow during that time. In a quiet desperation many of us resolved to live in a sort of tribute to his inspirational but short life.

Though younger than most kids in our group, Tom became ferocious in his dedication to live for the Lord. He got a lot of my time during his first couple of years in high school; less after that. I was pouring my time into Troy and aggressively investing in others who had not yet heard about Jesus. So while Tom continued to come to meetings faithfully, we didn't have as many personal conversations. Pretty soon his attendance became erratic. I thought nothing of it, assuming he was probably involved in lots of school activities. I took it for granted he would continue to represent the Lord well.

I was wrong.

Tom had dropped out of everything. He avoided me as much as he could. When I did see him and tried to engage him in small talk, he always kept moving. He never smiled or acted like we were friends or ever had been. At the end of the summer before his senior year, I decided I needed to corner him and find out what was up. I'd heard he was into a lot of self-destructive behavior. Friends of his—even his little brother—continued their involvement in my Campus Life meetings and all gave the same discouraging report: *Tom is in trouble.*

The grab-a-Coke-together meeting started awkwardly and never improved. Even though I used every crowbar in my trunk to try to pry info out of Tom, at the end I was left having to draw a lot of conclusions from his body language. He rolled his eyes when I told him I still cared about him. He snorted a disdainful laugh, shaking his head when I reminded him of the fellowship we'd shared together. And when I mentioned Dan's memory, he looked right through me—dispassionately.

"I hate God," he said.

I felt an incredible wave of guilt hit me. Somebody was *responsible* for this pain, and I was that somebody. I felt like I had failed Tom. I had stopped investing in him at the level I once did. I had taken him for granted. The rest of the conversation ended with a clunk, as I tried to find the words to apologize for something I instinctively knew I'd done wrong. In those days I made everything personal, diving into my evangelism efforts with passion and abandon. I would routinely set aside my own scheduled activities (or those of my wife) so I could respond in real time to the needs or interests of kids. But I'd let Tom slip away. *Yeah*, I reasoned later, *if Tom hates God, it's because I let him down.*

I didn't believe for even a moment that Tom really hated God. Tom began his journey with the Lord before his own developmental changes ushered in the doubts that so often naturally spring up during adolescence. His social life in high school followed the common trajectory of experiencing heightened temptations that come with age. And like a lot of people who hit valleys in their faith, Tom was not well equipped to handle the barren land of desperation after the growth and fruitfulness of his early Christian life. Nothing about God was working for him anymore. His anger, frustration, and self-loathing expressed itself as "I hate God"—but I wasn't convinced it was the totality of what he was feeling.

WHERE I STRUGGLED

So imagine you're me, sitting there as a student you love tells you he hates God. How would you respond? How do we help students when the tough times in their lives leave them wondering if God, or anyone else, really cares? How are we supposed to navigate our way through the pain that occurs when those we care about make deeply flawed decisions? Or to widen the net: When kids damage themselves, whether by their own choices or through no fault of their own, how should we cope?

> HOW DO WE HELP STUDENTS WHEN THE TOUGH TIMES IN THEIR LIVES LEAVE THEM WONDERING IF GOD, OR ANYONE ELSE, REALLY CARES?

I'm not going to say I failed in responding to Tom because I don't think I did. I kept trying; I stayed in his life; I sought the Lord on his behalf. But I did struggle. Greatly. Here's how:

1. I struggled with distance.

The ancient Greeks deliberated about how to respond to the pain and suffering we all inevitably experience. One group of philosophers concluded we should navigate through pain and suffering—ours or others—by arming ourselves with the *apatheia* of the gods. The resulting school of thought was known as *stoicism*. Even today a stoic person is one who's expressionless, one who follows that Greek tradition of responding to pain with apathy. Our culture thrives on this response. Keep others at a safe distance and don't get messy by letting their problems touch your heart. Many helping techniques advocate such an approach, recommending counselors maintain a professional distance for their own sakes. If our own emotions get all tied up in someone else's problems, we may not be able to offer that person much support. It makes perfect sense to those of us who've had airplane safety rules drilled into our subconscious. We need to put our own oxygen masks on *before* we try to help any child sitting near us.

This stoic Greek response completely fits my personality. I'm an analytical problem-solver. So in the face of one person's meltdown, I quickly moved to a systemic solution for all things wrong in my ministry. My immediate response is "What system can we put together to avoid this?" In systematizing the solution, I tend to miss the hurting heart sitting right there in front of me.

Jesus didn't do it this way. John reports Jesus' amazing response in the face of his friends' pain: *He wept* (John 11:35). No stoicism for our Lord. Real empathy results in real tears. And what's remarkable about these tears is that everyone would be jumping for joy within the hour. It could be argued that Jesus' tears were frivolous because he knew Lazarus was about to come back to life. That's not an argument I'd like to give an account for in heaven.

Jesus' response to the pain of Mary, Martha, and other false-starting mourners affirms an important, soul-saving posture for us in ministry. It's okay to feel and express sorrow as others are hurting— even if we know that what they *believe* is the problem is not *really* the problem.

2. I struggled with "failure."

Tom's expression of hatred for God came from a heap of hurt. And the amount of pain he was expressing rocked me back on my heels and left me feeling quite confused. I felt helpless to take away Tom's pain, and I sure didn't want to linger there. I wanted to move to solutions. My evaluation now, especially in light of Jesus' (unnecessary?) tears, is that my pain was right, and I should have embraced it transparently without trying to fix it. And, in my confusion over how to deal with Tom's hate, I blinked several times and struggled to accurately and adequately respond. And in that pause, which lasted a few months, Tom's problem got a little lost on me.

Maybe I struggled with how *pastoral* I should be. Do I sit back in my chair, listen to his pain, rub my chin slowly, and squint my eyes saying, "I see, and how does hating God make you feel?" Do I immediately tell him how wrong he is? Do I drop my head in my hands and weep in front of him? I just wasn't sure.

3. I struggled with balance.

In the midst of my own uncertainty, I felt Tom didn't get the response he needed from me. And that led to my making a few other inadequate decisions, which only left Tom feeling more neglected. It wasn't entirely my fault. With growing numbers of kids becoming involved in the ministry, I was feeling swamped. I was routinely working more than 70 hours a week, trying to balance my ministry responsibilities with what it meant to be a good husband in the first few years of marriage. Tom's harsh words were an indictment of me, of my inability to meet the expectations of others. It wasn't hard for me to conclude Tom really had needed more care or attention than he'd received from me. Unless I got my act together in ministry, I would surely disappoint others.

FINDING HOPE

In retrospect one big thing I believe I did right in this situation was trying. My flailing efforts were trying to access some wisdom I frankly had not yet attained. For instance: In my struggle to meet Tom's needs, management books became a source of hope for me. I tried organizing everything to the nth degree, seeking to gain control over every aspect of the ministry, trying to make sure this didn't happen to any other student in my care. One of the lasting benefits of this search for answers is I became a believer in the necessity of volunteers, largely because I had come face-to-face with my own limitations. My efforts in response to Tom were surely flawed, but I'm convinced that staying in the struggle—persevering—just *trying*—was a good thing.

IT WAS THE AMAZING, RELENTLESS LOVE OF GOD—CREATIVELY RESPONDING TO MY OWN NEEDS AS WELL AS TOM'S—THAT WROTE THE NEXT PART OF THIS SAGA. AND, AS ALWAYS, IT CAME IN GOD'S PERFECT TIMING.

The Lord taught me a lot through this experience. He taught me that my ways are not his ways. He routed his important lesson through my heart rather than my head, bypassing my normal inclination to dissect something to death. He reminded me of how much he loves surprises and how to trust him by praying and waiting for his perfect timing.

Henri Nouwen's book *In the Name of Jesus* offered a vital corrective to some of my mistaken thinking about managing my way through ministry. Such control is a myth and shouldn't be sought. In fact it is fed by one of the most dangerous temptations of ministry: The temptation to respond and meet people's needs without having taken those same needs before the Lord for his counsel. As the psalmist writes, "If God doesn't build the house, the builders only build shacks" (127:1, *The Message*).

It was the amazing, relentless love of God—creatively responding to my own needs as well as Tom's—that wrote the next part of this saga. And, as always, it came in God's perfect timing.

Here's what happened: I was praying in a sleepless way about Tom. Guilt was still a familiar companion, and every time I saw Tom, now a senior, I would toss and turn and cry out to the Lord. Tom was still unresponsive to me, but I believed there had to be a way to bring healing and hope to him, to restore him to the joy of his early days of salvation. Then the Lord gave me an idea for how I might reconnect with Tom.

At the time, the pope was visiting the United States and was scheduled to lead an outdoor mass in Chicago the next day. Knowing that Tom had been raised a Catholic, I called him and worked through some cool conversation to invite him to join me on a daylong road trip to be part of the experience. He would have to miss school, I explained, but I knew he'd been a fan of the pope and thought this might be a way for us to share a once-in-a-lifetime event. His enthusiastic response offered assurance that—in the words of Billy Crystal's character in *The Princess Bride*—Tom's spiritual life was only "*mostly* dead."

Chicago was more than three hours away, so we had a very long day together. It was fabulous, a 12-hour breakthrough in our relationship and a reigniting of Tom's interest in God. I don't mean to say that our relationship returned to what it had once been, but there was a new level of respect and understanding between us. More importantly Tom was on speaking terms with God again.

I haven't used the pope field trip as a youth ministry strategy again, but I have picked up a thing or two from this experience.

I've realized when I'm plunged into discouragement as I was by Tom's declaration, my tendency is to flail about and revert to my own style of coping. But I've become aware of this pattern, and I practice vigilance in guarding against it. Instead I earnestly seek the Lord for solutions—and I'm not surprised when God challenges me to abandon my thing to risk doing his thing. In doing this I almost unknowingly opened myself up to be healed from what ails me, including the injury of self-condemnation I'd heaped on my heart. God never tells us to do something for someone else without letting us taste its goodness ourselves. We really do find—and distribute—life-giving hope when we lose ourselves in the pervasive love and guidance of Christ Jesus.

Though I didn't realize it at the time, choosing not to believe Tom when he said he hated God was an act of faith, hope, and love. In faith, we can trust that nothing our students say or do surprises God at all, though their harsh words may cause our jaws to drop. In hope we can trust they're saying words they don't understand and, therefore, cannot possibly intend. Such hope always propels us to seek the breakthrough with a student, knowing that no one is beyond the reach of our loving heavenly Father. And in love we find the strength to stand and absorb the accusations, be they implied or explicit, fair or unfair. Love doesn't defend; it acts. Its immediate and timely response may only be tears, but that's okay. Though we can be certain God is up to something important in our students' lives, our love for those whose souls are contorted, confused, and even hateful will likely restrain our tongues so we choose simpler forms such as, "I'm so sorry," over weighty and ill-timed explanations.

I'm blown away that, as flawed as I am, God uses me. His sufficient grace has cemented hope in the center of my heart.

CHAPTER 5

WHEN YOU LOSE YOUR COOL WITH A PARENT

By Tim Baker

PERFECT. THE SITUATION WAS JUST ABOUT PERFECT.

Perfect church. Large congregation. Huge for me, really—about 2,000 people.

Perfect youth staff. A group of 30 hard-working, God-fearing, kid-loving, Bible-studying youth workers.

Perfect ministry. More than 500 kids attending our outreach events. Wonderful small groups fueled by an honest desire to learn about Christ. A congregation dedicated enough to give over an entire wing of the church building for student ministries. A budget that gave me freedom to spend funds on whatever I felt kids needed to grow in Christ.

Perfect. For me, it was the ideal church. I loved it.

That's why I thought a little backpacking trip into the mountains with our junior and senior high youth wouldn't be an issue. My plan was to challenge the students physically and, in turn, relate the challenge to their spiritual lives. So I figured I'd get them out in nature on a long hike. This kind of thing wasn't foreign to us. We'd worked hard in Mexico on mission trips. We'd spent hours doing service projects for our church. I figured hiking wasn't that big a deal. Besides, it was going to be an adventure!

From my vantage point, I did everything right. I communicated with kids ahead of time, giving them plenty of opportunities to ask questions. I did my best to map out the route wisely, choosing a relatively short, 20-mile round trip. We'd hike in 10 miles, camp and play for a day and a half, and then hike back out. To make sure I had all my boxes checked, I invited an experienced hiker to show me where to take the kids. We even made an initial hike to check out the route—just us two—and we had a grand time. I felt like I'd put a lot of effort into planning a great event.

I FELT LIKE I'D PUT A LOT OF EFFORT INTO PLANNING A GREAT EVENT. SO I WAS A LITTLE SURPRISED WHEN THE MOM OF ONE OF MY MIDDLE SCHOOL KIDS CAME TO TALK TO ME ABOUT SOME CONCERNS SHE HAD.

So I was a little surprised when the mom of one of my middle school kids came to talk to me about some concerns she had. Actually, she *confronted* me—and not in the privacy of my office. She caught me right next to our church's information center on a semi-busy midweek afternoon—right there where lots of people would see us talking. No, not talking—discussing.

Wait, not even that.

Emphatically sharing diverse ideas about how youth trips ought to be organized, planned, and pulled off. No, that's not it, either.

Okay.

Arguing.

Previously I'd only talked to this mom in passing—a "hi, howya-doin" kind of relationship. I remember glancing at her a few times after worship, nodding my head and smiling and her doing the same. She'd always seemed quiet, maybe even timid in how she expressed her feelings. When I'd overheard her talking, she'd never been loud or particularly noticeable. Not meek—just quiet in a controlled, reserved kind of way.

And that was how this conversation started—really calm: "Hi, Tim. I just wanted to double check a few things about this upcoming hiking trip. Do you have a minute?"

Honestly, I didn't. I keep a list of to dos for each day, and she wasn't on that day's list. So I'm sure I sounded a little put out, even though I did my best not to. "Sure," I said. "What's up?"

"Well, I want to know—have you thought about first aid on the trip? What if my son gets hurt?"

Actually, I had given it some thought. I had bandages on the trip list. See? That base was covered. But apparently that wasn't what she had in mind.

"I mean, do you have someone hiking with you on this trip who can effectively administer first aid?"

Obvious answer: No. Now, in my defense, I'd tried to recruit someone. But what nurse wants to hike 20 miles with a group of hyper kids? But I didn't figure my telling this mom, "There's not a nurse on this planet insane enough to make that trip," would engender a happy discussion.

So I responded with something more diplomatic: "I'm sure, as a parent, you'd feel safer if someone on the trip were trained in first aid. But at this point bandages are the best I can do."

I thought the strategy had worked because she moved on with: "What about drinks? How will kids keep their water bottles filled? It's hot—in my opinion, too hot for this trip. Have you found any clean water sources on the hike?"

Dang. She had me on this one. I hadn't.

Which is pretty much what I said, eliciting this response: "So I want to be clear on this: You're taking my son on a 20-mile hike into the middle of nowhere with no first aid, and you haven't even thought through the hydration issue. Are you insane?" She said this with one of those throw-up looks on her face—as if she'd just choked up a bit of the breakfast burrito she'd been eating in the car on the way over. I'm not sure, but I think she really did throw up a little in her mouth. Well, she made the face, anyway.

This is where things escalated a bit. Let's transport ourselves into the part of my brain ruled by emotions, shall we? When she implied I couldn't handle the trip, the little men in my head started banging on the inside of my skull with their tiny little sledgehammers.

I was peeved.

No, I was more than peeved. I was that other "p" word that good Christian youth workers aren't allowed to say. I got emotional and took the first line of defense I could think of.

"Are you aware of all the work this trip involves?" I blurted. "I've been doing everything I can to make this thing accessible to as many students as possible. If your son has issues with getting hurt or with drinking water, then maybe you need to think twice about sending him on this trip. You know, some kids just aren't cut out for this kind of experience."

I wanted to keep going and say something like: "And from what I know about your son, he really doesn't belong on a trip like this. Isn't he the kid who shows up for workdays and then sits 50 feet away from any work going on? In fact, maybe you're the one who should take a hike and hike your quiet behind right outta here. I think I can scare up your deposit. Wait here."

I didn't say that, but I'm pretty sure my face conveyed that kind of attitude, because her response was scathing.

"You know, I used to work with the students of this church," she snapped. (Actually, I didn't know that.) "I helped out our former youth pastor all the time. And when he planned trips like this, he was way more organized and worked to include everyone. It's too bad he isn't planning this trip."

Of course that made me really angry. Nothing gets under a youth pastor's skin like hearing about how great the previous youth pastor was. ("He knew way more songs on the guitar." "Her jokes were better.")

That was when I lost it.

I'm ashamed to admit it, but there, at the church information center in the middle of my perfect ministry setting, I argued for my qualifications to lead the ministry. I spoke about changes in leadership style. I made sure to throw in comments about capable students who contribute to student ministries and my ability to harness the "good kids" and draw them into the group.

When it was all over, I felt like Swiss cheese. I'd been shot through with effectively placed self-esteem-ripping comments. And I'd torn apart a relatively new relationship that should have flourished for the sake of an innocent middle school kid.

WHERE THINGS WENT WRONG

Moments like these test our true ministry skills—and I'm not talking about the abilities we have in event planning, Bible study teaching, or trip leading. These moments are like God's little checkups, showing us how we deal with deep issues—the hurting student, the emotions and fears of a concerned parent, and even our own insecurities. I've learned a lot from reflecting on the mistakes I made:

> NOTHING GETS UNDER A YOUTH PASTOR'S SKIN LIKE HEARING ABOUT HOW GREAT THE PREVIOUS YOUTH PASTOR WAS.

1. I let my enthusiasm take over.

When I plan a youth trip, I toss in as much activity as I can. If it's a mission trip, I make sure we have lots of fun planned. If it's a retreat, I put as much on the schedule as I can fit. If it's a simple Bible study, I usually have more material prepared than I have time to cover. And in the case of this hiking trip, I entered this weird, hyped-up-state where I felt like everyone needed to be included because the trip was going to be too good to miss. *Everyone* included all my students—even the middle school kids who were probably too young for such an experience. (I'd have probably invited kids from the nursery if I'd thought about it. We could have tied them on our backs.) So, yeah, enthusiasm—it took over, and it kept me from acting with appropriate caution.

I should've thought more about the abilities of my younger students, looked at weather forecasts for the area during that time of the year, sought out more trip leaders, and consulted with key parents before I announced the trip. There's something to be said about not rushing to move forward with big events. I should've done my homework and been more cautious.

2. I didn't explain the trip adequately to students and parents.

At youth group I gave broad generalizations about the trip. I mentioned things like "getting away from your parents" and "hiking up high into the atmosphere" and "sleeping under the stars." However, I failed to mention words like "20-mile journey" and "packing and carrying your own stuff" and even "it rains often where we're going."

This same inadequate explanation carried over to the parents. The material I sent home contained the same general information—just enough to get parents excited, not enough to make them feel secure about the trip. That lack of info made the trip seem like an excellent idea for all students—even the younger ones who probably weren't ready for such a grueling trek.

3. Instead of listening, I responded to the mom's concerns with anger. Blinded by my enthusiasm and protective of my event, I stonewalled her. The minute she questioned anything about the trip, I was indignant.

Did I have a right to be indignant?

Heck no.

The trip wasn't about me or my grand plans. It was about her kid. And her responsibility was not to affirm whatever I'd planned; it was to make sure her kid was safe while in my care. My lack of specifics made this mom feel the trip was an accident waiting to happen—and in fact, that's exactly what it was. On our first night on the mountain, it rained buckets. As we tried to escape the next day, we were trapped. Tiny streams from the day before were now raging rivers. Solid ground had become mushy mud, difficult to cross. Many of the younger hikers often gave up as we slowly moved down the soaked mountain.

Her questions were valid: Was everything in place to make sure all the students were safe? Was the event really appropriate for her son? Would he be able to keep up with the older students? Was there any possibility he'd get hurt? But her legitimate questions were met with my attitude. How dare she question my planning abilities? I started the escalation of emotion and anger. The big blow up was really my fault. Had I not responded with anger, I might have built a better relationship with both this mom and her son. As it turned out, the mom took her kid to another youth group, and I never saw them again.

I not only failed to explain the event effectively, I also failed to respect her role as parent and listen to her concerns. So I really was wrong on two counts, both in what I planned and in the way I responded to her.

4. I internalized her criticisms.

To be honest, after she told me how she felt, the whole trip lost its luster. I proceeded with the hike, but I didn't enjoy it as much as I should have. I spent the entire time wondering who else I'd hear from before the trip was over. Maybe I really had blown it and, in that case, maybe I didn't have the necessary skills to take a group this size on a trip this difficult.

> THOSE NEGATIVE THOUGHTS, PLANTED BY HER WORDS, BEGAN TO RULE MY MINISTRY. I WAS CONSTANTLY LOOKING OVER MY SHOULDER AND WAITING FOR THE NEXT ANGRY PARENT.

When she talked about how much she'd appreciated the previous youth pastor, I translated that internally as "You're bad at your job, and you're worthless." She wasn't saying that, but that's what I heard. Even though I argued with her, the criticisms stayed with me for quite a while. Those negative thoughts, planted by her words, began to rule my ministry. I was constantly looking over my shoulder and waiting for the next angry parent.

5. I didn't call on other parents or my pastor for wisdom and support.

When this mom leveled me with her comments, I didn't bring other parents into the conversation. I really needed other parents I could call and ask about the issues she was raising. Had I miscommunicated? Did I cast my net too wide, including students who were too young? Did I provide enough information about the trip? Having other parent confidants would also have allowed me to get more information about this angry parent, too. Was she difficult with others? Were there additional issues I wasn't aware of?

Parents have the right to offer their opinions about the way we're working with their kids. They have the right to express concerns or even complain. But they don't have the right to tear us apart. We aren't punching bags for parents to jab at when they're in crisis. We aren't doormats. Having more parent friends in my corner assures that, if this ever happens again, I could easily get the perspective of someone else involved in the youth program.

Similarly, I could've used the support of another ministry professional in dealing with this situation. My pastor would've probably
helped out a lot here. Actually, in the middle of our disagreement, I
should have said, "Let's go and talk about this with our pastor. I know
he'd like to help us resolve this." I should have drawn on his professional experience and pastoral wisdom.

6. I never sought reconciliation.

Maybe the worst thing about this argument is I never said, "I'm sorry."
I never accepted responsibility for the way I reacted. I never asked
for her forgiveness. When we were done yelling, I went back to my office and she headed out to her car. It was up to me to smooth things over, and I didn't take advantage of that opportunity. And that mistake, perhaps even more than my initial reaction, ruled out the possibility of my having any continuing ministry with this family.

PARENTS AREN'T
OUR ENEMIES. THEY
DON'T NAIL OUR
PICTURES TO THEIR
CLOSET WALLS AND
THROW DARTS AT
THEM. THEY DON'T
SPEND THEIR DAYS
TRYING TO FIGURE
OUT NEW WAYS TO
WORK AGAINST US,
EVEN THOUGH IT
SOMETIMES FEELS
LIKE THEY DO. BUT
JUST BECAUSE
THEY'RE NOT OUR
ENEMIES DOESN'T
MEAN THEY'RE
ALWAYS EASY TO
WORK WITH.

FINDING HOPE

Ultimately, parents aren't our enemies. They don't nail our pictures to their closet walls and throw darts at them. They don't spend their days trying to figure out new ways to work against us, even though it sometimes feels as if they do. But just because they're not our enemies doesn't mean they're always easy to work with. Parents can be demanding, and they can be difficult.

When I began working with students, I thought something I've heard many other young youth workers say: "I've never parented teen-agers, but I've spent enough time with them to know what it's like to raise them." Now, as my own kids reach their teen years, I realize how wrong that rhetoric is. Working with students isn't anything like raising them. I do love the kids I work with, but I only have to love them for a few hours each week. Parents have to love them at all times, through all things, and in all situations. That includes when they puke, when they rage, and when they weep; when they're difficult, when they're funny, and when they're not.

I've learned from being a parent and from having my own kid in someone else's youth group. I now know what it's like on the other side of the ministry fence, and I have a much better sense of what that mom was probably feeling the day we had our conflict. Ultimately parents are just looking out for their kids. Think of them as protective lions always on the lookout for anything that might harm their young. It's their responsibility to watch out for their kids. Sometimes that protectiveness comes out with barbs and thorns. Other times it comes out calmer and quieter. Looking back, I realize that mom was just trying to do what all parents want to do—both protect their kids and allow them to try out experiences that will stretch and grow them.

> STAY COMMITTED TO YOUR RELATIONSHIP WITH PARENTS. REMEMBER THEY'RE YOUR BEST ALLIES IN REACHING THE HEARTS OF YOUR STUDENTS.

When parents get in your face, you've got a tough choice. You can ignore their concerns, rebuff their suggestions, and question their intentions. But I have to tell you, that can create big problems. Ultimately if we choose to be jerks when we interact with concerned parents, it can severely affect the relationships we've worked so hard to establish with their kids.

If you've experienced significant conflict with the parent of a kid in your ministry, you need to remember this: You're not ministry trash. In fact, you're normal. "Iron sharpens iron," the saying goes. It doesn't say "A cushy pillow shines up a pink feather." Relationships, especially ministry relationships, can be tough. How can we learn to work through conflict constructively unless we actually experience conflict? Who's better to teach us about dealing with parents than the parent who's a little too picky and overprotective?

Don't lose hope when you come into conflict with parents. Stay committed to your relationship with those parents. Remember they're your best allies in reaching the hearts of your students. It's not enough to tolerate them—you have to love them, too. Even when it feels impossible. And especially when you mess up.

CHAPTER 6

WHEN YOU FEEL WORTHLESS

By Danette Matty

I CLEARLY REMEMBER THE DAY I GENTLY CONFRONTED my friend Rob about the frustration some parents and leaders were feeling about his work ethic. That day taught me some invaluable lessons about timing and bouncing back after being sucker-punched.

Rob and I had begun following Jesus around the same time in our respective lives. We sometimes shared stories about the "colorful" pre-Christ years we'd experienced while we were both in the military. We became close friends, and I deeply respected that he now brought the same passion for God and students as he'd once brought to living in sin.

We fell out of touch for years, only to end up serving the same church, where I was a volunteer and he was the youth pastor. Rob was still passionate, but a little more arrogant than I remembered. He understood youth culture, knew how to train leaders, and was an incredible communicator—and he knew it.

On the day I sat in Rob's sports-themed office, I wanted to help him realize some folks in the church were unhappy. I knew he wasn't the sofa spud some people there believed him to be. So quietly and privately, I approached Rob and gave examples of calls he'd not returned and reasonable times he'd not been available when people needed him to be. I hoped our long friendship would allow him to hear these concerns without getting too defensive.

Did Rob bow and thank me for being a messenger sent by God? Did he cry out, "Thank the Lord, my God, that I have a loyal friend like you, watching my back"?

Nooooo.

He looked me directly in the eyes and said I didn't "have a voice" in his life and shouldn't concern myself with things that were none of my business.

I was stunned.

My face froze but my mind raced. None of my business? I wanted to say, "It's my business because everyone knows we're friends, and since you're too cocky to approach, they all come to me!" But my weak spine was still in training back then, so I pushed back with all the courage of a stuffed teddy bear, then slinked out when he took a phone call. I sat in my car for a few minutes, feeling both hurt and angry for the way he'd spoken to me.

But it wasn't just about being offended and hurt. Rob made me feel worthless. My opinion meant nothing to him, despite the count-less hours I was pouring into this ministry each week. Apparently it was okay for me to tell Rob the good things I saw in his leadership and how much I supported his ministry, but the minute I said any-thing critical, even in a respectful way, he pushed the mute button.

To Rob's credit, he later apologized for snapping at me. But I knew I still didn't have the coveted "voice" in his well-guarded life. The feelings of worthlessness continued.

That backfired attempt to challenge Rob wouldn't be the last time he made me feel less than mint. I led our youth-adult worship team. Three of us rotated the leadership for our youth worship service. We weren't Hillsong United, but no one covered their ears when we played, either. Yet Rob would come to me almost every Wednesday after the service and tell me what was wrong with so-and-so's worship style—and occasionally I was so-and-so. Or he'd tell me this or that song wasn't connecting with half the students. Even if that meant the other half liked the song okay, that wasn't enough.

We couldn't win. One of the worship leaders threatened to quit if Rob didn't back off. People can only take so much constant criticism before they either begin to believe they're just not cut out for it, resent the critic to the point of being unteachable (even when good advice is offered), or become overly critical of themselves. As it happened,

Rob took another ministry position and moved before we could stage a coup.

Rob isn't the only person who has made me feel worthless during my 20 years in youth ministry. Although most of my students have been a joy to shepherd, there have been a few who have done a real number on my self-esteem.

Like Trina, for example.

Trina was emo before emo was fashionable. She didn't smile; she glared. She didn't pout; she sulked—especially when interacting with our female leaders. Still, I reached out to her as I would any other girl in our ministry and tried not to mirror back her snotty attitudes. But all I got were glares and one-word staccato responses, no matter what I asked her—be it "How's it going?" or "How are things at school?" or "Would you like to stab me?"

By then my spine was a little sturdier. I wasn't going to beg Trina to open up, but I wasn't going to stop reaching out to her, either. Then one day I showed up for a small-group backyard party. After hanging out for a few minutes, my co-leader casually pulled me aside. He told me he'd gone up to Trina and asked how she was. She shot back, "I'll be fine as long as Danette doesn't ask me how I'm doing."

Are you sure you don't just want to stab me?

At that moment, all my youth ministry experience and relational skills went out the window. In that moment, those old feelings of worthlessness resurfaced. I backed away and tried to be kind when I saw her. I never let Trina or too many others know how much her continual rejection stung. I was the big person. Kids shouldn't be able to hurt adults like that, right?

In times like that, I want to run up to the difficult student and yell, "Hey, ain't nobody paying me to take time away from my family to give you a jingle! It's because I actually care about your pointy little head!" What do these kids assume—that we youth leaders are trying to rack up points with God? Well, okay, maybe some of us think we're doing that. But, for the most part, we've got this God-thing inside us that compels us to give a rip. So we call. We ask how they're doing. And we really want to know.

I'm thankful there were enough other students who needed and wanted my attention; one tough kid's barbs didn't invalidate my worth. So my self-esteem was still in one piece when I stepped in as the interim director of youth ministry at our church.

Although I've had invitations to interview for full-time ministry positions, I've spent most of my youth ministry career as a committed volunteer. With two children at home, my desire to keep the best of both worlds intact has made volunteering the best choice for me. But when our much-loved youth pastor announced he was moving away to be closer to his family, I felt a strong sense the Lord wanted to use me to step into a larger role that would prepare our ministry for its next director.

The team was supportive of me and enthusiastic about what we were doing. We tightened up our program and sharpened our leadership skills. We all felt good about the changes we were making. So I was surprised at the stress and job-performance anxiety with which I struggled. Satan, the enemy of our souls, specializes in morphing those feelings into worthlessness.

When our senior high guys began to trickle away from youth group, a couple each week, it was discouraging. I really cared about those students, and they knew it. Even though we'd inherited a small crop of seventh graders (one of the excuses the senior high guys used for their leaving), our group shrunk while I, the 20-year veteran, was at the helm. Hand me that magic marker so I can draw a big "L" on my forehead!

I told everyone, including myself, I wouldn't go crazy logging long hours. I wouldn't sacrifice my home life or the paid freelance work I depended on for income. What a joke! My weekly one-on-ones with my children went out the window. For the first time in my writing career, I got behind on deadlines. But now that I had the clout to really make some changes in the ministry, I found it hard not to overwork. Here was my chance to implement some things I felt were important. I was free to take excellence to the nth degree.

My friend Brian told me that his wife, Kristi, was in the same position—which he described as "part-time pay with full-time ownership." When student ministry is your calling and you actually enjoy it, it's hard not to overwork—not just in the hour-logging department, but in the desire for excellence. I'd been part of a large, well-run ministry. I'd witnessed the effective administration of a youth group and experienced the fun of programs that served people and not the other way around. That's what I wanted.

But I also wanted to attend students' events.

And develop adult and student leaders, with regular training and mentoring meetings.

And make regular jaunts to the public school down the street, building relationships with faculty and meeting students for lunch.

And schedule regular service projects to help students obey the biblical mandate to serve the poor and feed the hungry; to help kids extend their God-view beyond their social periphery.

And—well, do I really need to continue with the list of worthwhile things I'd like to have done, all of which would have contributed to a thriving student ministry?

I knew those things would be best accomplished when I had the time, resources, and volunteers to support that level of intention and programming. They can't be done piecemeal, a couple of hours here and there, every other week, with no budget and a handful of volunteers who all have their own lives. And unless you have clear instruction from the Lord, it's arrogant to assume you can manage a 20-volunteer, 200-body, big-budget program when your actual capacity is a third of that. That's the difference between visionaries, pragmatists, and people who've been around the youth ministry block a few times.

I knew all this in my head. But it didn't stop me from obsessing over what wasn't being done, particularly what wasn't being done by me. I didn't act on my "not enough" feelings because I could see God doing cool things in students and leaders in our shrunken group. And it helped that, after months of consistent team prayer and follow-up, those fickle seniors trickled back in, even bringing friends. Yet I spent the whole year struggling with guilt, vacillating between the fulfillment that comes with obedience to God and the frustration that comes with our own unfulfilled ministry hopes.

I SPENT THE WHOLE YEAR STRUGGLING WITH GUILT, VACILLATING BETWEEN THE FULFILLMENT THAT COMES WITH OBEDIENCE TO GOD AND THE FRUSTRATION THAT COMES WITH OUR OWN UNFULFILLED MINISTRY HOPES.

WHAT I DID WRONG

Feelings of worthlessness can have many sources—whether it's negative feedback from a colleague in ministry, attacks from students to whom we've reached out, or disappointment at our own ability to reach our hopes and dreams. As I've reflected on the situations that have caused me to question my own worth, I've realized how my own mistakes have contributed to those feelings:

1. I was a wimp.

Okay, it's not that simple. But consider the situation with Rob, who lashed out at me when I tried to offer him some constructive criticism. I had great intentions, I just wasn't willing to pay the price that might come when he wasn't receptive to what I felt he needed to hear. I wasn't secure enough to say what needed to be said non-defensively and guilt-free. Eventually I got the memo that you can be honest, direct, and even confrontational while still being kindhearted and even-toned, walking away with your self-respect intact.

2. I tried too hard to keep everyone happy.

As one of my mentors, Jeanne Mayo, says, "You have to be willing to be hurt." There were many times when I tried too hard to be a friend when the other person really needed me to be a solid, confident leader.

When it came to my time as interim director of the ministry at my church, I knew I couldn't do it all. But I felt an overcooked responsibility to set a better-than-best example if I expected volunteers to step up. I put more pressure on myself than anyone else did. So when crises arose, we got through them—but I brought more hand-wringing stress on myself because I wanted to make everything right. And my stress left me always feeling like I needed to do something more to shrink the conflict or make someone else feel better.

I also personalized people's criticisms. I'd been part of well-run leadership teams and youth ministries. I wanted so badly to contribute I took it personally when people didn't assume my motives were the purest or my advice the wisest.

3. I should've been more secure in my position as a Spirit-led leader and sought the Spirit for truth more regularly.

So often our instincts are right but we don't know how to act on them. That's why we need to rely on God's Spirit tenaciously. The Holy Spirit is secure in his position and wise to prompt us when to speak, when to bide our time, or when to be quiet. We need to learn to obey his prompting rather than being led by our own emotions or egos.

A friend once taught me the simple prayer, "Jesus, tell me the truth about this." There are times in ministry where we all feel like some part of us is on the line—whether it's our hearts, our egos, our street credibility with students, or our reputations with other leaders and parents. In the midst of those moments when misunderstanding and hurt are so common, we've got to step back—mentally, emotionally, and sometimes even literally—and pray, "Jesus, tell me the truth about this so I don't react from some false premise or assumption." Satan works in darkness and lies. Jesus works in light and truth.

FINDING HOPE

In my youth group many years ago, there were two teenage girls I used to call or spend time with nearly every week. These girls were always together, and I tried to get to know both of them and encourage their faith development. I know that one of the girls, Lucy, used to joke with her friends about that "religious lady" who called her every week. She would humor me with good manners, but Lucy never really opened up.

But Lucy's friend Liz was a different story. She was hungry for more than what weekend partying and a verbally abusive boyfriend fed her. So when I'd call her, she'd actually talk about herself, life at school, her family, and her boyfriend. She began to grow and blossom into a solid, engaging young woman of God. I continued to speak into her life even after high school.

A few years later when Liz was home on a break from college, we met for coffee. She shared about how she was leading a Bible study for the girls in her dorm. After she relayed a couple of stories of sharing her faith and supporting the girls in her group, I almost teared up. I told her how proud I was of her for mentoring them. She commented something to the effect of, "Well, I learned from the best."

> OUR EFFORTS FOR GOD ARE NEVER WORTHLESS, EVEN WHEN WE FEEL LIKE THE SEEDS WE PLANT ARE BEARING LITTLE FRUIT.

Liz's words offer me more than a nice ego boost. More importantly, she reminded me that we reap every little thing we've sown. Our efforts for God are never worthless, even when we feel like the seeds we plant are bearing little fruit.

Remember Rob's continual displeasure at the efforts of our worship team? I never really believed we were as inept as he'd said. After all, each of us had been leading worship in various other venues for years, receiving appreciative feedback. I knew we were doing good work. Yet under Rob's disapproval, it was hard to remember that.

Around that same time I got a phone call from the pastor of a large church in another state. He wanted to fly me out there once a month to lead worship for a start-up ministry. He said, "Danette, you were always one of my favorite worship leaders. I just love your energy!" When I mentioned that it seemed like quite an expense for him to fly me out, he said, "Well, if I go to the board and say I want Danette Matty to lead worship for this ministry, money is no object."

You can't imagine how big my head swelled. My cheeks were splitting. How I'd relish telling Rob I wouldn't be around one Wednesday a month because I'd be flying out to offer others the same expertise he was too superior and demanding to value!

Alas, that vision never got past the *Fantasy Island* stage. I gave that pastor an alternate idea for his worship team that was both more cost-effective and community-oriented. (My ego is occasionally balanced by wisdom.) But the Holy Spirit has used that phone call to remind me of my own God-given value and to stave off the Worthless Worm.

Should I allow my sense of worth to suffer under the scrutiny of a leader like Rob whom I could never please? Or do I let my ego balloon because another leader tells me, "You have what we need, and I'm willing to go to any extreme so you can bring it to us"?

As I considered those questions, I sensed the Lord saying to me, ever so simply: "You do exactly what I tell you, and you do it for me." It couldn't have been clearer.

Those words God offered me are the words I want to share with others who struggle with questions about their own worth. You'd better know exactly what you're called to do, because you can't please everyone. And you'd better do it with the target of pleasing God. I love how Proverbs 16:7 takes it even further, telling us, "when people's lives please the Lord, even their enemies are at peace with them" (NLT).

If you're working in youth ministry, some people will be critical of your gifts, leadership style, and decisions; others will be enamored. Which of these people should you try to please?

Neither. Please the One who called you, not the ones to whom you're called. In him we live, move, and have our being—and so much more. That's our worth.

CHAPTER 7

WHEN YOU'RE FIRED

By Len Evans

A LONG, LONG TIME AGO IN A CHURCH FAR, FAR AWAY as a padawan youth pastor, I had a utopian view of what it'd be like to work in youth ministry. When I began my first youth ministry job, I half-expected we'd sing "Kum-Bah-Yah" when we closed our staff meetings. Turns out I had no idea what to expect. It's one thing to envision yourself in an ideal church, in a job that's just one spiritual high after another. It's another to experience life in a real (also known as the non-ideal) youth ministry setting. Every youth ministry position I've served has had some way in which it was atypical and less than ideal. And one of those positions, as it turned out, was just plain painful.

My first ministry job was great, but not easy. I had a few good years there. I didn't get fired, but I was "helped" out of the position after the pastor and I had a heart-to-heart in which I shared that the role I was serving in (the role of Christian educator, also overseeing 10 ministries with an emphasis on the youth ministry) wasn't the best fit for me or the wisest way to structure the ministry. He affirmed me and my calling, but encouraged me to begin looking.

Although that conversation was healthy, the fallout wasn't. I was shocked a week later when another leader's wife asked my wife about us looking for a new ministry. Wasn't that confidential conversation I'd had with the pastor, uh, confidential? And, even though I'd not been fired, the pressure to find something in the next six months began. Ironically, the person hired after I left was given a different job description that focused entirely on youth ministry. So maybe I did make a difference there after all.

"Helped" out of a position. Strike one.

My next job was a perfect fit. I oversaw a large youth ministry that grew while I was there. But eventually I learned all it takes is one person who really doesn't like you. That person can build a campaign that will wear down even your greatest supporters. I was once stopped in the hallway by someone I barely knew who asked me, "Is she still trying to get you fired?" It was comments like those that encouraged me to look elsewhere before it came to the point where they officially fired me.

One angry person out to get me. Strike two.

You'd think those two negative experiences would be enough. I'd been helped out of one position by the pastor and driven from a second by someone eager to get rid of me. A pair of uncomfortable exits from ministry positions that, apparently, I wasn't called to stay in for more than three years. My hopes that youth ministry would always be a loving, disaster-free experience had been dashed. I began to fear being known as "the three-year guy with a limited bag of tricks."

WHAT KIND OF CHURCH MOVES A FAMILY ACROSS THE COUNTRY AND THEN SAYS, "SORRY IT DIDN'T WORK OUT, STAY WARM AND WELL FED," AFTER TWO AND A HALF MONTHS?

But that didn't keep me from diving back in. A position opened up clear across the country and, while the move was a stretch for my family, the position seemed ideal. I was asked to oversee the children's, youth, and family ministries—all areas I felt comfortable leading. The church was constructing its first building, and I agreed to work another job while volunteering ten hours a week to the high school ministry. Despite the fact that I had been in full-time youth ministry for more than 10 years, the position was labeled an internship for the first six months. But after my six-month internship I was brought on board full-time. It was great to finally be settled.

I was fired after less than three months. There were no moral issues. I hadn't done anything wrong. It was simple: The senior pastor wasn't happy with me. I didn't meet his expectations, so I was gone. My family and I were totally devastated. What kind of church moves a family across the country and then says, "Sorry it didn't work out, stay warm and well fed," after two and a half months? Three of the six elders shared this sentiment with me separately: "I didn't agree we should fire you, but what could we do? We're just elders."

One upset pastor. Strike three.

At that point I really began to wonder: Was I out of the youth ministry game? Maybe I hadn't heard God before and he had to do this to get my attention. It was almost too much. How do you recover from something as huge as moving across the country just to get fired?

We took about a month off. We didn't go to church. We struggled to pray. When our family did pray together, most of the prayers were short and shallow. How do you pray after this? Thinking about what happened was painful. I lost 16 pounds over the next five to six weeks because of stress and not wanting to eat. We just wanted the pain to stop.

In *Getting Fired for the Glory of God*, Mike Yaconelli wrote, "I'm beginning to believe that if those who are called into youth ministry follow the lead of the One who called them, getting fired is inevitable." I felt a sense of vindication as I remembered Mike's words. Maybe I was the one who was right, and the real difficulty was that the church didn't even know what God's voice sounded like. We don't live in an ideal world but rather a fallen one, and that means there may be times when good youth workers get fired for no good reason. At the same time, I knew that some firings are justified, whether they're due to character issues, rebellion against authority, or simply not having the skills necessary to do the job. But whether the reasons for our firing are clear to us or not, losing one's job creates a crisis of confidence.

After I was fired I worked some temporary jobs to fill in the financial holes. I wondered if God would call me into another church. I didn't want to be out of youth ministry, but honestly I knew enough about walking with God to know I'd only be happy if I followed wherever God led me. If God's path carried me away from youth ministry, I'd go, but I couldn't say I'd be thrilled.

RIGHTS AND WRONGS

Even as I wondered what God would do, I gave a lot of thought to how I'd handled these three ministry positions. It was clear I'd made some mistakes along the way. To be honest, it's not easy to disclose my ignorance or the things I've done wrong. Does *anyone* really like telling others where they've messed up? However, if talking about my mistakes will help others who struggle with similar issues, it's worth it. So as I reflect back on those situations, I can see a few things I did wrong:

1. My idealism led to unrealistic expectations.

Yep, I'm a "perfect world" person. I believe we can all live together in peace and harmony. That belief has ruled some of my ministry through the years. And looking back, it was a liability that caused me to be blindsided by the realities of ministry life. Church leaders are mostly good people, but they're still imperfect and carry their own emotional baggage.

My idealism also blinded me to the reality that some people in the church lie. Seeing that for the first time was like getting punched in the face. Churches are often too "nice" to be straightforward about the reason for your firing, or they may feel like they need to cover their rears. So rather than firing you, they may inform you that they want a resignation letter. If you resign, it's easier for church leaders to explain your departure away to the congregation as "the Lord was leading elsewhere." They may even make a severance offer to you with the understanding that you'll be less-than-up-front in talking with people about why you left. Sure, it is blackmail—but it can also mean a few weeks or months of guaranteed income, which can feel pretty important when facing a potentially long job search. Be wise about what agreements you make, and don't lie to get money. But carefully consider whether you can agree with what they want you to say without violating your conscience.

2. I forgot how little things can add up to big things.

You've heard the phrase about "the straw that broke the camel's back," right? Well, that applies everywhere, including the ministry.

And in the ministry, that last straw can be anything. An angry parent can be that one-too-many straw. The kid who continues to disobey and gets in trouble on a retreat can snap the back of the camel. The pastor who makes you the object of his or her dissatisfaction can bring that metaphor to life. Sometimes the last straw is just some little habit you have that someone else finds annoying.

I'm the kind of youth worker who doesn't follow up on every little pet peeve someone shares with me. I don't go out trying to solve every problem I hear of in order to add another notch to my ministry belt. I tend to be very flexible and have a "whatever" attitude regarding a lot of ministry issues I don't see as vitally important. That can annoy people I work with and for. People want their youth leaders to address their pet peeves, to see and solve any and every problem they might call about.

So when I got a call about *whatever*—the student who wasn't obeying his parents, the leader who wasn't teaching the right way, the retreat next March that I hadn't completely planned yet—I sometimes brushed off those concerns. I put them in my *deal with later* file. Looking back, that didn't suit the personality of the student ministry or the church. They needed more than I offered them. Did they need a babysitter? Should I have wiped every runny nose? I'm not sure that's even a healthy ministry model, but still—I probably should have given those calls more attention.

I've learned that when someone shares something with us that might sound like a little thing, we need to try to hear it through that person's ears. If the concern is important enough that someone takes time to share it with you, you probably shouldn't assume it's no big deal. It may be an issue you need to address and try to fix, even if it's not your highest priority. It's like leaving the dirty dishes out one night. It really isn't a big deal in most marriages, but if you say you're going to clean the kitchen and the dishes are still there every morning, eventually it's going to become a big deal.

3. I believed everyone shared my vision for students.

I thought everyone viewed the ministry the same way I did. I assumed the kids who came—the ones who were important to me—were equally important to everyone in the church. I assumed even the rough kids—the ones who wore black, smoked, or were a bit too emo for other churches—would fit into our ministry with no complaints by the leadership. So when about 10 of those kids starting coming to our meetings, I expected everyone else in the church would be as happy about it as I was. I was thrilled those kids felt comfortable enough to keep coming to our worship and discipleship program. They weren't angels, but they were earnest in their questions and 100 percent authentic—perhaps too authentic for a few people. Not everyone in the church was thrilled that "these kids" were "influencing *our* kids."

My mistake was in not helping the other students and their parents see the opportunity that was before us. These new kids were seeking Christ in a real and lasting way. Certainly nobody in the church hated these kids, but a few parents were uncomfortable with their being part of the group and influencing their children. I should've done more to calm the irrational fears of some of our church people.

4. I wasn't the right fit.
I've been in enough churches to know matching the personalities among the members of a church staff is important. Ministry can be a very personality-driven animal, and when personalities clash, you've got problems. It's part of the Five-Star Fit scenario I've written about in other publications. There has to be a good Professional Fit (the job itself), Cultural Fit (the community or region of the country), Theological Fit (agreement on more than just the big issues), Philosophical Fit (the same strategy for ministry), and Personal Fit (the personalities of those working together).

Looking back to the interview process, the church team and I asked the right questions of each other. We were truthful. We shared our passion accurately. I was careful and they were, too. But nothing prepared either of us for the clash of our personalities. I didn't realize that who they were and what they valued were different from my own identity and values. And yet my personality was such an awkward fit for them that it became one of the chief reasons they let me go.

FINDING HOPE

When I was fired from the third ministry position, I didn't give up—but I sure wanted to. I questioned God over and over, wondering if this kick in the pants was also a kick out of student ministry. I didn't know if I needed some time away or if I needed to step away for good.

If you're a youth worker who gets fired or is asked to leave a church, it can mean more than just the loss of a job. The lost income may result in a feeling of economic instability for you and your family. You may lose trust in the larger church and other Christians because of the way the local church or ministry handled your situation. Your firing may cause you to question your own value and sense of identity. All these are very real dangers and ones I struggled with. But I'm happy to report I did do a few things right during these difficult times:

I left with grace.

Even though I probably had a right to tell others the ins and outs of the situation and the injustice I was facing, I didn't. I kept the gory details away from the rest of the church. I didn't take down the leadership when we disagreed nor did I try to lead others away from the church, even when I thought the situation was unhealthy. So I have no regrets about how I left.

If you're forced out of a church, do your best to leave with grace—even if you feel the church doesn't deserve it. If you were unjustly fired or asked to leave, people will know. Good character will overcome any misinformation, half-truths, or outright lies that may be thrown around after your departure. If you've already left a church in a way that lacked grace, you can still "leave with grace" by going back to the leadership, apologizing, and rebuilding the bridge.

I have a friend who showed a great deal of grace when he left a church more than 10 years ago. When people would dig for more information about the "real story," he refused to drag the church down by sharing the little things (or big things) that annoyed him about the church and its leadership. Today he's back on staff at that very same church in a different role. You never know what opportunities might arise if you leave gracefully and avoid talking trash about your former church.

I reached out to others for support.

I followed the advice of a close friend and connected with other people who were close to me—the network of people whom I loved and who loved me back. I shared my story and told them I needed prayer, encouragement, support, and love. Who better to provide that care for us than our families and close friends?

I also reached out to other youth workers because I needed the camaraderie I'd experienced at conventions, over meals, and at other youth worker gatherings. When we've been hurt by a church, it's a good idea to connect with friends in ministry because, odds are, our friends who've spent any significant amount of time in ministry have also taken the "red pill" themselves and discovered some of the less pleasant realities of the church matrix. Other youth pastors can offer true empathy to you and remind you why you answered the call of ministering to students in the first place.

I'm blessed to have a vast network of friends who work in a variety of roles and ministries. I sent an email to most of them within a month of being fired (once I was ready to come out of my personal cave), and I was so grateful for the support I received. I also was very fortunate to find a new church to attend where the pastor was a true shepherd to me. He loved me, let me rant, prayed for my family and me, and played a big role in our eventual healing.

I embraced my grief.

You've probably talked with more than a few hurting students or sat through classes on the psychology of grief. If so, you'll understand what I'm talking about when I say grief is like a long, dark tunnel. At times the darkness can be overwhelming.

The emotional effects of being fired are similar to going through a divorce or losing a loved one. In her 1969 book *On Death and Dying*, Elisabeth Kübler-Ross proposed people progress through five stages when dealing with any kind of grief and tragedy: Denial, anger, bargaining, depression, and acceptance. Moving through those stages is important in order to fully recover and move toward a healthier life.

I walked that tunnel and embraced each stage. It took me a little over a year, and maybe in a way I'm still walking out of that tunnel. The time each of us spends in that tunnel will vary depending on a variety of factors, yet it's a journey each of us must make in order to move back into wholeness. Write the five stages of grief on a 3 x 5 card and carry them with you or put them on a post-it note in your car or on your bathroom mirror. Monitor your progress through those stages in the same way a diabetic monitors his blood sugar level.

I relied on God the Provider.
The church treasurer may sign your paycheck, but God is the provider. Maybe all the negative ministry experiences I've gone through were simply to teach me that one lesson. Apparently, of all the things God has needed to teach me, this was one I had to learn the hard way. Despite a master's degree and 10 years of ministry experience, I found myself waiting tables, digging ditches, and handling a 90-pound jack hammer for four to six hours a day—hard times for a guy who expected a career filled with weekend lock-ins and mission trips.

But knowing God was my ultimate Provider led me to more diligence. I learned God had other opportunities for me; I just needed to stay obedient and follow where he led me. I got to work doing jobs outside youth ministry, and they led to other ministry opportunities. Yeah, I worked a jackhammer—and I had opportunities to tell the other guys working jackhammers about Jesus. Trusting God meant relying on him to lead me to ministry outside of "ministry." My foreman asked questions about my faith. My kids experienced a side of their dad they'd never seen before. I gained friendships I never expected. I learned I needed to trust God more than I trusted my résumé. And all that learning happened while God allowed me to continue to bring in a regular paycheck.

When the tough times come, it really doesn't matter how long you've been in ministry, which seminary you went to, or whether you went to seminary at all. What matters is this: Are you trusting the always faithful God during this time or not? When we pivot from trusting in ourselves to trusting in God, it brings a peace that is difficult to explain. We can find ourselves strangely content in circumstances that might have seemed impossible just a few weeks ago. That contentment comes from trusting in God's plan and will and not your own.

Learning to place my trust in God was far from the only lesson God taught me through these experiences. In my time of crisis, those old, familiar, foundational truths of the faith—things like the importance of prayer, the power of forgiveness, and the centrality of love—found new meaning in my ministry life. They didn't just help me weather the storm of the event—They took deeper root in my soul and became a part of my character more than ever before.

I'd never want to relive those days, but I know God used that time to change me. I can honestly say I've learned to really love the local church. I still believe, even with all her warts, the local church is the primary way God has provided to help and love a dying and lost world. That theological stake helped me reconsider youth ministry as a vocation. I gave some thought to other positions within the church, but it was my conviction that youth ministry was what I could do best to make God smile the most. I made a decision to remain in youth ministry, and I'm thankful to be caring for students in a local church setting again.

If you're between ministry positions, pray and hope for the right job, but do more than that. Get to work and be thankful for anything God provides for you. Whatever work you do, you can do it for the glory of God. God is our Provider, and, by the way, Jesus said something about the birds of the air and the lilies of the field you might want to keep in mind.

I've also learned this: The pain will end. It's impossible to know exactly how long the pain will last or when it will end. But through the pain, the wisest choice is to hang on to God and allow him to hang on to you. During my dark night of the soul, I felt a deep longing to remain close to God despite feeling as if he might not be there. God was with me in my time of darkness, and he's with you now. In the times of struggle when God is all we have, we realize that God really is enough—that he really is our ultimate Hope.

CHAPTER 8

WHEN YOUR OFFICE IS A WRECK

By Rick Bundschuh

THE PHONE CALL AWAKENED MY FRIEND CRAIG AT 2 a.m. He answered groggily.

"This is the Sierra Madre Police Department," said the excited voice on the line. "Are you connected with the church?"

"Uh, um, yeah, I'm the janitor, and I also teach the college age group," mumbled Craig.

"Well, I think you should come down here to the church right now. We think we foiled a burglary in progress."

"Whoa, yeah, okay, I'll be right there!" shot back Craig, the news having now awakened him completely.

"What is it?" said Laura, Craig's wife, as he fumbled in the dark for his pants.

"Cops called. Somebody broke into the church," said Craig.

> I THINK YOU SHOULD COME DOWN HERE TO THE CHURCH RIGHT NOW. WE THINK WE FOILED A BURGLARY IN PROGRESS.

As Craig drove his beat-up old truck the mile or so to the church where he and I both worked, his thoughts raced, wondering what a thief would find so compelling in the church. There was very little cash, but there was some office equipment and audio-visual gear that might be pawned for a few bucks.

The red lights twirled in the quiet blackness as Craig pulled into the church parking lot. *It's amazing the cops didn't wake up Rick. He lives right next to the church*, Craig thought.

It was true. I was serving as the church's youth pastor and living in a church-owned house no more than 40 feet from the back door of the church kitchen. But I'd been sound asleep, blissfully unaware of the excitement next door.

Craig followed the flashlight beams and came upon a few police officers who were obviously excited. Not much happens around this small town, and they were thrilled they'd interrupted a crime in progress.

"Our patrol officer noticed a door ajar," one cop reported to Craig. "He decided to enter the premises to check things out. The thief must have heard him and made a run for it out another door." It was clear from his rapid speech the officer's adrenaline was still racing.

"Can you tell what was stolen?" asked Craig.

"We don't think they took anything," said the officer. "We must have surprised them. But they were obviously looking for stuff. We interrupted them while they were ransacking one of the offices."

"Do you think someone is still hiding in there?" asked Craig.

"No, we're pretty sure they made a run for it. But let me show you what we found," said the officer.

Craig and the cops made their way upstairs.

"This is the office they ransacked," said the policeman. "Look at the cash they left stacked on the desk. They must have run when they heard us coming. We found the door slightly open."

Craig peeked into the office.

Papers littered the floor and desk, books lay open and disorganized all over the room, empty Dr. Pepper cans were scattered around, two overflowing trash cans were leaned up against the wall, photos lay strewn about the floor, and money was stacked in several random piles on top of the desk.

"See? Ransacked!" said the cop.

"Yeah, it sure looks that way," Craig replied.

"We probably scared them away just in the nick of time," the officer beamed.

"I bet you did. Thanks for being on the job," Craig said.

The officers congratulated one another on a job well done and drove off with spotlights blazing, hoping to find the culprit hiding behind a dumpster somewhere.

But Craig knew the truth.

There'd been no burglar in the office that night. Craig knew my office always looks as if a bomb has just gone off in it. He knew the money scattered about the desk was most likely the deposits for an upcoming youth camp we'd been promoting. He figured I'd probably thrown the deposits on my desk at the end of the day and then forgotten to close the door tight on my way out.

In short, Craig knew it was the youth director himself who had trashed the youth director's office.

An hour later Craig was back in bed thinking of ways to get revenge against me for a disrupted night's sleep.

Whatever irritation Craig might have had soon dissolved with the knowledge that he now had a perfect excuse to needle me for the rest of my life.

He played his cards real cool when I bumped into him the next day.

"Guess what happened last night?" he offered casually, adding, "And boy do you owe me for this one!"

Then he told the story. Within minutes we were laughing heartily (amidst my profuse apologies) about the sincere but mistaken cops, an office that actually looked as if it had been ransacked, and Craig's tongue-biting attempt to keep from dousing the cop's enthusiasm with the cold water of the youth pastor's slobbery.

Needless to say I gave my office an immaculate cleaning that very day. But it didn't last. Pretty soon things were a shambles again.

Now, let me explain a couple of reasons why my office tends to be such a mess.

One is that I am, by nature, somewhat of an environmental slob. When it comes to paperwork, magazines, books, and other clutter, I can live with disarray for an amazing amount of time, especially if I'm multitasking or in the throes of a project or an event.

The slob routine doesn't transfer to every part of my life. I'm a two-shower-a-day, brush-and-floss, use-deodorant, minty-fresh-breath kind of guy—but I can live in extreme office chaos without flinching.

I'd argue that this is genetic, or at the very least a product of early social conditioning—a lived-too-long-without-a-mother kind of thing. Some of us seem predisposed to clutter by nature, and that probably includes you if you're still reading this chapter. (The anal-retentive types probably skipped this chapter since they would *never* allow their workspaces, countertops, garage floors, or trash cans to be anything but spit-and-polish clean.)

And I do have a method to my disorganization. I know it *looks* messy and chaotic, but this is just an illusion. The piles all over my office may seem random, but I have a pretty good idea which pile contains the thing I'm looking for. Put this stuff in a filing cabinet and then I'd be really lost.

Perhaps my story helps you feel like less of a failure despite the fact that your office was recently declared a federal disaster area. But there's another explanation—and if you're like me in the way you approach youth work, you know it's the *real* reason why our offices tend to be messy dumps.

It's because that little square space with your name on the door isn't really your office. You see, we youth workers don't do most of our work sitting behind desks. Our offices are our cars, the ball fields, the beaches, the slopes, the skate parks—wherever kids hang out.

Our filing systems are in our glove compartments and back pockets.

Our memo pads are ink on our forearms.

Our secretaries are our cell phones.

Our desks are in front of our laptops.

Our office hours are "whenever."

That little room at the church? Well, we visit it from time to time. Maybe one day a week we do a little work behind the desk and show our faces to other staff members who never leave their offices. But we're more likely to race in and out (sometimes trailed by a host of kids), wearing shorts and a T-shirt as office attire. For the most part, our offices are dumping grounds—storage places for basketballs, finger shockers, bizarre hats, whoopee cushions, and toys. We don't spend a whole lot of time there because the kids we've given our hearts, time, and energy to don't keep office hours or even come to offices.

Unless they're trailing us, kids don't usually see our offices. They don't make appointments and then wait in the hall for us to get done with our previous client, as if we were psychologists or something. Those kids who do visit us at the church don't want to sit in our offices (unless there's something to play with); they want to know if there is anything to eat in the church refrigerator. They don't even bother to ask—they just help themselves to the pie that was put there for the women's Bible study tomorrow morning. Then they come into your office to eat and leave leftovers or dirty dishes stashed under a chair for the ants to clean—implicating you in the theft of the pie.

Of course, none of these realities comes off real well if a parent or some other church member stumbles into the shambles of your office.

GETTING INTO THE MESS

It's pretty obvious I made a big mistake in failing to lock the door of my office on the night the police discovered the "break-in." If I've got cash from the youth group's trip deposits scattered about my desk, it's only sensible to lock my office door. And in terms of the general mess, as the saying goes, not everything that *can* be revealed *should* be revealed.

Notice I didn't say my big mistake was not having a clean office. Having an office that's always clean may not be altogether practical for some of us. (As I plunk out these words, I'm looking at chaos surrounding me that's begging to be put in order regardless of my deadline, a lunch appointment, kids to pick up, and a "honey do" list. But I should've tried to take at least an hour or two every other week or so where basic house...er, office-keeping could be done.

It would also have been helpful if I had communicated to other staff about the "nature" and true purpose of my office. For co-workers who virtually live in their own offices, the chaos of my office might seem to indicate a shoddily run youth ministry, an undisciplined leader, and a poor steward to boot. And those assumptions could lead to some negative comments or even an attempt to bring the boom down on us in some way or another. (Of course, any attempt to explain *why* one's office is a disaster is best done *before* the cops are called in to check out reports of the vandalism; otherwise, it is likely to come off as a pathetic excuse.)

I'm going to assume for most of us with trashy office syndrome, the clutter surrounding our desks doesn't indicate huge problems with our stewardship, self- discipline, or quality of our work. But what else can we do to protect our reputations and our ministries from self-incrimination or the darts of other well-meaning neat freaks?

When I actually cleaned my office, I should've made the most of it. I could've hosted an open house for everyone else on staff complete with sparkling cider and hors d'oeuvres so they could see the miraculous transformation I had wrought with my own hands. Then I could lock the door again and let it dissolve back into chaos.

I also could've arranged to get some help from someone in the church or even youth group who had the "gift of organization" and who would see an office like mine the same way mountain climbers see Everest. With a little bit of advertisement, I could have made all of us happy.

CLEANUP TIME

If you find yourself lying awake at night fearing that the cops may be writing police reports about the messy state of your office, here's my advice to you: Fergetaboutit!

A dirty office is really the least of your concerns.

Your concern is hanging out with students, caring about kids, and developing relationships with staff and teens in such a way that you can leak Jesus into their lives.

Your concern is to make sure your busy schedule allows time for your family—time to stomp in the mud with your children and to make love to your spouse (but not necessarily in that order).

Your concern is to find balance in your personal life. Pursue a hobby, sport, or pastime that has nothing to do with youth ministry—so you can be fresh for doing ministry.

Your concern is to be sure you have some place of solitude where you can escape and meet with Jesus without being distracted by a phone ringing, people coming by, or the specter of a desk that needs to be tended to.

I know the big mailing needs to be sent out, the money for camp counted and turned in, the contact list updated, the Bible study materials duplicated, and the office straightened up. But in terms of your priorities, an intimate walk with God, a happy, healthy family and personal life, and a relationship-building type of ministry far outrank whether your office is a trash pile.

> AT THE END OF ALL TIME, WHEN JESUS IS HANDING OUT THE "WELL DONE, GOOD AND FAITHFUL SERVANT" CERTIFICATES, I DOUBT HE'LL BE GIVING OUT HONORS FOR KEEPING ONE'S OFFICE NEAT AND TIDY.

And take solace in the fact that those youth workers who do hover in spotless offices are often not doing a lot of youth work. They may be doing a lot of organizing, administrating, paper shuffling, and so forth—and some of them may even be doing effective ministry. But it is doubtful there are throngs of kids eagerly awaiting the opportunity to come and hang around their offices and get into their well-organized files.

At the end of all time, when Jesus is handing out the "well done, good and faithful servant" certificates, I doubt he'll be giving out honors for keeping one's office neat and tidy. But it wouldn't surprise me if there weren't a few awards presented to youth pastors who spent so much time loving kids that their offices were never shipshape.

CHAPTER 9

WHEN THE EVENT FAILS

By Jason Raitz

I STILL REMEMBER THAT MOMENT AS IF IT WERE JUST yesterday. It was 3 a.m., the grass was wet with dew, and the generators were still purring in the background. I was standing in an open field, looking at a massive stage where bands had been playing for the last two days. I remember thinking how big that stage was—and how incredibly small I felt.

My stomach was queasy, my head was throbbing, and my eyes felt like they were on fire. I was absolutely exhausted, and my body felt like I'd been run over by a very large truck. My throat was dry from all the yelling—and I'm not usually much of a yelling person. But that night, I was yelling at God at the top of my lungs, screaming with every ounce of my being. And to make matters worse, I just couldn't stop crying.

> I FELT LIKE MY LIFE WAS OVER—AND NOT JUST MY MINISTRY LIFE, OR MY LIFE AS A YOUTH PASTOR. MY ENTIRE LIFE.

I felt like my life was over—and not just my ministry life, or my life as a youth pastor.

My entire life.

I was embarrassed, humiliated, broken, and shattered. I didn't know which direction was up. To be completely and utterly honest, part of me hoped I'd fall asleep that night and never wake up.

That's how I felt when my event failed.

Now, every youth worker has experienced failure of some kind when it comes to events. We plan and plan and nobody shows up. We pray and pray that 35 kids will sign up for the mission trip—and only 7 do. We work and work to get ready for a big outreach event, only to find out there's a huge basketball game the same night and nobody is coming.

Failure is hard, no matter the size. When we fail to meet our own or others' expectations, or when the outcome of something we've worked toward is the opposite of everything we'd hoped, prayed, and planned for, it can take us to our lowest places and force us to look at ourselves in pretty vulnerable ways.

My big-failure story starts in my living room on Thanksgiving break of 2004. I'd gathered together a few close friends, and we'd decided to start a nonprofit ministry that would train junior high students to love God and others passionately and provide practical help and encouragement for youth pastors. We felt like we had pure motives and the best of intentions. We decided to kick off our new ministry with a big event that would bring students together, rally local churches, and hopefully raise additional funds to get the ministry going.

With that, Blitzfest was birthed. It was a two-day music festival featuring five stages, a children's tent, a seminar tent, a skate park, a professional skate team, a dozen inflatable events, a gigantic merchandise tent, a few hundred volunteers, dozens of speakers, and more than 60 bands.

Now, I know what you're thinking: Why would you plan something so huge as your very first event? (You *were* thinking that, weren't you?) And you're right—it was a huge undertaking. We had to rent a local park and then bring in all the power, all the staging, all the sound, all the lighting, all the water, and all the tents. Money needed to be raised, permits needed to be pulled, insurance had to be bought, and—most important of all—we needed to get the word out. So, yes, it was a big event for our first one.

But you need to understand two things about me: First, I love events. I fell in love with them while working at my first church, and I've continued to have a deep affection for events. Call me crazy—but I've always been someone who attends every event I can—just to scope it out. I love to think about an event's strategy—the details, the promotion plan, the program, and the purpose. Some people build models for a hobby; I attend and dream up events. It energizes me.

I love starting with a blank whiteboard and envisioning an event that has the possibility to create momentum for a ministry, to get people involved in serving, and to create experiential moments in which students make life-changing decisions for Christ.

The other card in my pocket was the fact that I had 10 years of experience planning "successful" events. I know that sounds arrogant, but up until then I'd really only experienced "success" with events. I'd pulled off dozens of concerts. For 10 years and at three different churches, my team would plan and execute an annual lock-in that doubled in attendance every year. The final year we hosted the lock-in, we'd expected about 1,000 kids to attend—and we had to shut down registration at 2,200. It was great to have that many kids show up, but the way God truly put his hand on that event was even better. At my next church we hosted a number of one-night events that exceeded all expectations and drew amazing numbers of students. So even though this particular ministry was brand new, we felt like we had the experience necessary to pull off Blitzfest. For our team, it seemed like a reasonable risk to plan something this big.

We started planning the event with great energy and passion. The members of our team poured their lives into starting this ministry and making the event all it could be. At the time I was still a full-time junior high pastor at a large suburban church, a position which demanded a great deal of my time. On top of that my wife and I had a new baby (our third child), and we'd recently found out he had a genetic disorder that would require an incredible amount of extra time maintaining his diet.

One night my wife woke me up because she was in excruciating pain. I rushed her to the hospital, and we found out she had more than 70 gallstones and needed to have her gall bladder removed. The surgery required a huge incision and left her with a tube in her side for the next three months. She couldn't lift anything because of her surgeries and could barely walk. She was unable to hold our baby or take care of our other two kids. Needless to say it was a really rough time! I was trying to be Mr. Mom, trying to be a good youth pastor, and trying to get our new ministry off the ground.

Are you tracking with me?

Despite all this, I knew, without a shadow of a doubt, God wanted me to start this ministry and plan this event. I heard his voice. I had a calling. I had a great peace knowing I was living out God's will for my life. And despite how busy I was, everything seemed to be going smoothly. We hosted our first fundraiser, formed a board of directors, and sent out the first promotional pieces for the event. We'd even had some churches register. It was all coming together.

Or so I thought.

Until that phone call came. I can still close my eyes and take myself to the place I was standing when that phone rang. I even remember exactly what time it was: 3:33 p.m.

It was my friend and ministry partner. I'd known him for years. We were very good friends with like minds and similar entrepreneurial skills. He was a worship leader and I was a speaker. I worked full-time at one church, and he worked part-time at another church. We'd planned a half dozen other events together that had all turned out great—very successful events. With this new ministry, we'd decided he'd handle the logistics of the ministry (because he had more time available), and I would be the connector (with youth pastors and donors) and the primary communicator.

The moment I answered the phone, I knew something was wrong. His voice quivered as he began to tell me a story that made my knees buckle. Because of some family issues, he needed to step down from his role at his church and our ministry. It was a major crisis, and I was deeply saddened.

So let's pause for a quick recap:

My ministry partner and I founded a brand new nonprofit ministry that was planning a massive event.

I was still working full-time as junior high pastor of a church where I was required to lead three services each weekend for our students.

My wife and I had three kids, including an infant with some extra needs.

My wife got sick and was out of commission for a few months.

My ministry partner stepped down from our ministry and his church, and his family was hurting and struggling.

This was the biggest event I'd ever planned.

I had some major decisions to make. I knew my responsibilities at church were too heavy for me to continue while taking on the logistics of this new ministry and the work on this event. We had a newly formed team of volunteers who had faithfully given their time and finances, and they were all looking to me and the board to make a decision. After spending time praying, meeting with my board, and talking with the leaders at our church, I decided to leave my position at the church so I could get this new ministry and Blitzfest off the ground.

It was an extremely tough decision! But an incredible peace rushed to my soul after I made the decision.

We continued to work. We raised money, built a Web site, hosted lunches for youth pastors, and cast the vision to leaders, churches, and anybody else who would listen. And we prayed.

We prayed for beautiful weather—both days were gorgeous.

We prayed for volunteers—many served.

We prayed for donations—funds poured in.

We prayed for youth pastors to commit to bringing their students—they committed.

We prayed for unity among our ministry team and board of directors—we had it.

And we prayed for a certain number of people to attend—*and they didn't come.*

They just didn't come. We didn't reach our expected attendance and it crushed us! In order to break even we needed about 3,500 people to attend. We had hopes we might have far more than that. But in the end, Blitzfest drew about 1,200 people.

The result? I couldn't honor the financial obligations for the event. And I wasn't just a little bit short on funds. I was facing a six-figure loss. Yup, you read that right—*six figures!* It's the kind of debt I'll be repaying for a lifetime.

So maybe you can understand some of what I was feeling that night as I stood in that field at 3 a.m. It's still hard for me to take myself back to that moment mentally and emotionally. I can't fully explain everything that was running through my mind. Pain. Humiliation. Worry. Embarrassment. Shame. One feeling I remember quite well is something I'm very embarrassed about and afraid of. It's hard for me to even type it out. But on that night I did let the awful thought of taking my own life creep into my mind.

My team members and I had spent thousands of hours preparing. We prayed fervently. We believed. We hoped. And even with all that, the number of people we needed to attend just didn't show up. By my definition of failure (when you don't meet your own expectations, or the expectations of others, or when the outcome of your work is the opposite of what you had hoped for and planned), Blitzfest had failed.

> THERE WAS REALLY ONLY ONE BIG QUESTION PULSING THROUGH MY MIND THAT HOT JUNE NIGHT: WHAT WENT WRONG? I JUST KEPT SCREAMING THAT AT MYSELF— AND AT GOD.

WHAT WENT WRONG?

There was really only one big question pulsing through my mind that hot June night: What went wrong? I just kept screaming that at myself—and at God. WHAT WENT WRONG? What did I miss? Even though we had great intentions and we thought we had pure hearts; things didn't end up how we dreamed they would.

It's been nearly three years, and I've had a lot of time to process some of my thoughts on what went wrong:

1. My life wasn't balanced.

My wife was sick and recovering from surgery. We had three children, and our youngest had a genetic disorder we were just learning about. I had a full-time job as a youth pastor at a large church that involved lots of responsibilities. I just didn't pay attention to my life—my boundaries and my limitations. How could I think I could add one more thing to a plate that was already overloaded? How could I take on another big challenge and expect to keep my life in balance? How could I possibly give my family, the church, and the new ministry the attention they all deserved?

2. I was blinded by pride.
For 10 years I thought I was the greatest youth pastor of them all. I felt like I could do anything. And I believe my heart's deepest desire was to reach kids for Jesus. But with all those years of "success-ful" events, my pride had grown incredibly large. When my partner backed out, I should have made large adjustments that would have scaled down the event. Instead I let my pride rule. I thought "I can do it all—I can grow this ministry and plan this event myself and it will be successful." Embarrassingly enough, I actually remember having daydreams of thousands of people showing up.

3. The event was too big and too much.
If I could go back in time and change only one thing about the event, I'd go back and scale down the event—drastically. My dreams were bigger than reality. This event we'd envisioned was massive. We need-ed to promote it, we needed to organize it, and we needed to raise money. For a first-year event, it was simply too big. A lot of events fail because of poor planning, but not this one. It was planned really well for a first-year event. It was just way too big and way too much for our first event.

4. We had the wrong target audience.
I promoted the event primarily to other youth pastors in the area. I assumed they'd get excited about bringing their students to a two-day concert with 60 Christian bands. I was wrong. The youth pastors in my area weren't interested in bringing their students to a festival filled with bands. I should have searched out my audience sooner and realized it wasn't the youth pastors I needed to reach, but the teenag-ers in my area.

MOVING FORWARD AFTER THE QUESTION

When an event you've planned doesn't meet your hopes and expectations, it's essential to ask "What went wrong?" But you can't ask that question forever. You must move on.

With every failed event there are lessons to be learned. If you're like me, you'll probably have a list of things you'd do differently if you could. But the reality is: It's over. You can't undo the past. You can't change it. You can either dwell on it or move past it. If you dwell on it, you'll be crippled by the failure, and you may miss the lessons God is trying to teach you.

Of course, letting go is definitely easier said than done! I've been working diligently for three years to try to move past this event and learn the lessons God has for me. For the first year after Blitzfest, memories of it haunted my dreams and I thought it about it constantly. It's taken me a long time to process everything that happened. One thing I've come to realize is you can never truly overcome failure. It's a part of life. What's important is how you're going to walk through it and recover from it. Here are several lessons I've learned about walking through failure and recovering from it:

Ask for help.
Cry out to God. Fall at his feet. Lay down your pride and hand it over to God. Pray that your heart and your pride would be shattered, and then find your strength in God. Take encouragement from these words: "Is anyone crying for help? God is listening, ready to rescue you. If your heart is broken, you'll find God right there; if you're kicked in the gut, he'll help you catch your breath. Disciples so often get into trouble; still, God is there every time" (Psalms 34:17-19, *The Message*).

Take one day at a time.
This is so simple to say, but so hard to live. Remember it will get better and it might have been worse. I think of Proverbs 3:5-6: "Trust God from the bottom of your heart; don't try to figure out everything on your own. Listen for God's voice in everything you do, everywhere you go" (The Message). Give God each moment and make each day an

experiment of faith. Remind yourself this failure doesn't define who you are. It's not final. Each day is a new day.

Remember your source.

One reason the failure of my event hit me so hard was because I'd built my identity around my years of producing "successful" events. I saw myself as the guy who could bring out the big attendance numbers and get lots of hands in the air. My identity was based on what I produced and not on being a child of God. Colossians 3:1-2 (*The Message*) says, "So if you're serious about living this new resurrection life with Christ, act like it. Pursue the things over which Christ presides. Don't shuffle along, eyes to the ground, absorbed with the things right in front of you. Look up, and be alert to what is going on around Christ—that's where the action is. See things from his perspective." Those verses remind me that my identity is based on who God created me to be and not what I produce.

Get a reality check.

Blitzfest was a colossal failure from a financial standpoint. But the event actually had some great moments. For a long time all I could see were the negatives. But I've spent some time over the last couple of years trying to force myself to see and write down all the awesome parts. For example, the people who attended the event—they loved it. They were excited about it and really hoped it would happen again. They emailed and called to let us know how much those days impacted their lives. The event was well organized and programmed, especially for a first-year event. We worked hard, and in many ways we did a great job. But because of the weight of the financial failure, I was unable to see the ways it had been a success.

Celebrate the God moments.

One of the big-name bands and the generator company forgave our debt. Each of those was definitely a God moment! Students were encouraged, our volunteers served, and God was honored. It's so easy to forget about the God moments when the shadow of failure seems to cover so much territory. Even when things aren't all we'd hoped for, we need to make sure we take time to celebrate the God moments.

Avoid the "what ifs."

It's been more than three years, but sometimes I still get caught up in the "what ifs." What if 2,500 people had attended? What if 4,000 people had attended? What if I would have scaled it back? What if my partner hadn't had to back out? The "what ifs" will continually take your breath away and paralyze you. So don't give in to them. Learn the lessons you can and move on one day at a time.

Don't give up.

Failure is an incredible journey! I love being a youth pastor and I still love events. I really do. I still believe big events have the potential to do great things for God.

I don't know the scale of your failure. My failure was huge and humiliating—big enough that I thought I was done with ministry altogether. In the weeks and months that followed, I battled daily with thoughts of wanting to quit or give up.

But I didn't quit. I kept moving forward. I was so incredibly blessed to have a great team of people around me who loved me and helped me walk through that difficult season of life.

For a long time I thought I'd never plan another event. But God had different plans for me. Whatever failure you've experienced, remember failure is not the final word. Trust God and continue to listen to his voice. Live one day at a time. And don't give up.

CHAPTER 10

WHEN CRISIS RULES THE MINISTRY

By Adam McLane

HOOSIERS.

You know the movie, right?

Norman Dale, a successful college basketball coach with a checkered past, moves to a small farming community in Indiana and takes a job coaching the high school team. But from his very first day on the job, Dale struggles with credibility. He's an outsider, and the town can't stand him. The school's best player doesn't want to be on the team; the other players are undisciplined. His only friend is the school principal, who stays busy trying to stave off the onslaught of naysayers pointing out the coach's every character flaw. Norman Dale knows how to coach a team; he is expertly trained and experienced. But he also knows establishing credibility will be difficult.

His first day at the school is memorable. The principal walks him down the hallway to the school gymnasium. As he steps into the gym and gets his first look at the guys he's been asked to turn into a team, Coach Dale blows the whistle and mumbles to himself, *"Let's see what kind of hand I've been dealt."*

I've experienced similar scenes in my own journey. At significant moments in my ministry career some authority figure who believes in me enough to give me a shot has led me down the hallway to a new group of students, said some nice words, and then walked away. And in that moment I've thought to myself, *Let's see what kind of hand I've been dealt.*

Haven't all of us been in Coach Dale's gym? Don't we know how it feels to look at a new group of students and feel them looking back at us for the first time? Haven't we all faced an abundance of problems and been forced to confront our own fears and personal demons on our way to leading our ministry team to "victory"?

We're qualified, trained, and we've experienced success. While our jobs might not come with trophies, huge incomes, or notoriety, we're still winners. But none of that prevents the, uh, well...the stuff from hitting the fan from time to time. In fact, to be honest, it's not a question of *whether* it'll hit the fan; it's more a question of *when*.

Yeah, you know it's going to happen. Will you have the skill to respond to the splatter in a manner that allows victory to become a reality in your situation? That's the more important question.

I accepted my first volunteer position in youth ministry while I was an undergraduate student at Moody Bible Institute. The pastor in charge of the senior high ministry of a local church needed help organizing events and overseeing the large number of students attending. I was excited about the opportunity. I was confident in my ability to help Larry. And I felt this position could be an important experience for me as I approached vocational youth ministry.

On my first day, I arrived 15 minutes early and glided eagerly to the third-floor offices. I was bursting with excitement—I don't think my feet even touched the ground. As I opened the door, Larry was hanging up the phone. He looked at me and grimly said, "You need to go downstairs to talk to the family pastor."

I had no idea why.

Was there paperwork I needed to fill out? Was I getting a raise already? Unfortunately, it wasn't anything like that.

Larry told me he'd just been fired. With that news, my heart sank into my shoes. Larry was my good friend, and I'd really looked forward to working alongside him and learning from him. But clearly that wasn't going to happen.

I can still see the pain in Larry's eyes. The awkward questions were right there, completely visible on his tired face. *What was he going to do? How would we tell all the students?*

I didn't know what to say. After a few seconds, I finally said, "So how are you doing, Larry?" It was a completely useless question, but it was the only phrase my confused mind could shape.

"Fine," he said blankly. "I should have known it was coming."

I closed the door, swallowed hard, and made my way to the family pastor's office. I said a few quick prayers. I prayed for Larry and the awkward place he was in. I prayed for the students. I prayed for the church. And I prayed the Holy Spirit would get me through this meeting.

As it turns out, the church had come up with a different plan for my internship. I was asked to lead the high school ministry on an interim basis until they could hire someone new. For the next couple of weeks they needed me to take on all the administrative aspects of the job. Then, after the news Larry was leaving became public, I would take more of a leading role as he transitioned out. I'd be expected to organize and lead the group, with a primary focus on setting up the volunteer team and students to accept a new senior high pastor in about six months. In that instant, my job shifted from something I felt relatively prepared for—providing support to a seasoned youth pastor while being mentored by him—to uncharted waters of leading a ministry through a dramatic shift.

> IN THAT INSTANT, MY JOB SHIFTED FROM SOMETHING I FELT RELATIVELY PREPARED FOR—PROVIDING SUPPORT TO A SEASONED YOUTH PASTOR WHILE BEING MENTORED BY HIM—TO UNCHARTED WATERS OF LEADING A MINISTRY THROUGH A DRAMATIC SHIFT.

Despite how this whole event rocked my friend Larry, I saw it as an opportunity for everyone. Larry was getting out of a ministry that didn't fit him, and he'd have a chance to step out into new ministry waters. For me, it was an opportunity to actually lead a student ministry—something I'd wanted to do and something I'd been training to do, even though it was happening way earlier than I'd expected. And honestly it felt like a chance for the church to grow as well. Larry had been struggling, and it was probably time for new leadership. Maybe the church was turning a corner, and maybe I was the guy to help make that turn. Had I been handpicked by God to lead them through this transition?

I closed my eyes, held on tight, and hoped against hope.

But soon after I accepted this new leadership position, things went downhill. Larry, hurt and looking for answers, began to tell volunteers his side of the story. And in his fragile emotional state, it probably wasn't the wisest choice.

The more he shared, the more the ministry was rocked. It wasn't long before our volunteer group of 20 adults began to disintegrate. These leaders were angry and frustrated over how Larry's firing was handled. Many of them wanted to quit, and those who wanted to stay were asking hard questions about what had happened. They wanted answers. Some of them trusted the church leadership and felt the church had made a tough but critically important decision. The rest of them—well, they were less than fully convinced. They were mostly suspicious and seemed unwilling to listen to the stories of everyone involved.

That's what was happening among the staff in our ministry. But as the news spread, things got messier. Anger and frustration started to spin out of control. As Larry attempted to complete his final duties, bitterness began to creep into the youth group. People were uncertain. Was Larry okay? What would happen next?

When Larry's last workday and good-bye party came, there was a great sense of relief. We were finally able to begin moving forward. We'd made it through the emotional loss and political minefield. Now we were ready to begin the hard work of setting up the next guy.

But not so fast. Before we could get too excited about moving in a new direction, there was the excruciating work of trying to figure out how things had gone so wrong.

DISSECTING THE CALAMITY

There were lots of potential suspects I could blame for things falling apart. I could blame Larry and the volunteers who continued to support him. I could blame the parents. Or I could blame the senior pastor and the church leadership committee who ran the whole show. Let's take them one by one:

It's the fault of the youth workers, right?

Shortly after Larry was fired, I called a meeting with all the youth ministry volunteers. As we sat around the table of a local restaurant munching on sandwiches, these leaders poured out their hearts. They were devastated about what had happened to Larry, and they were ready to fight the church leadership over it. Together they were crafting a shared story they would tell their friends and relatives about what had happened. And that story placed the blame on the church leaders.

I knew these ministry volunteers felt devastated about what had happened. Yet all their complaining reminded me of the biblical story where the wandering Israelites want to blame all their problems on Moses and Aaron:

> The whole community was in an uproar, wailing all night long. All the People of Israel grumbled against Moses and Aaron. The entire community was in on it: "Why didn't we die in Egypt? Or in this wilderness? Why has God brought us to this country to kill us? Our wives and children are about to become plunder. Why don't we just head back to Egypt? And right now!"
>
> Soon they were all saying it to one another: "Let's pick a new leader; let's head back to Egypt."
>
> Moses and Aaron fell on their faces in front of the entire community, gathered in emergency session. (Numbers 14:1-5, *The Message*)

As these disgruntled youth workers and I gathered in our own emergency session, I was tempted to tell them they just needed to trust the people in charge. I wanted to say what I thought a good church leader should say: "You should trust the leadership; they've made a good decision. We're your leaders and God has called you to follow us." I wanted them to be good little sheep, to blindly trust me, and to let me take the reins and lead them. But as the meeting unfolded, I recognized I'd need to adopt a different strategy if things were going to get better.

But maybe the youth workers weren't the problem. In fact—

It's probably the angry parents' fault.

As I sought to lead the students and staff into a new era, I began to understand more about the difficult situation I was facing. Parents were quick to gripe about tiny details. Students were always pushing the limits and boundaries of our ministry, seeking to challenge every detail and deadline we set. Some loved Larry, so nothing I did would ever be as good as what he did. Others just wanted to challenge us, as if it was their mission to make us uncomfortable about every deci-sion we made. It was, um, crappy.

In the midst of all this unhappiness, we were planning an event that required all students to register with cash so we could hold their spots. To make a long story short, several students missed the dead-line. This might not be a problem for most youth ministries, but it was a problem for us. The previous youth pastor had often allowed students to slide in past the deadlines, but this had caused several previous events to sink deeply into debt when places were booked for students who never showed. And the numbers for the event we were planning were really soft—we didn't know if we had 60 or 120 students coming—which made things difficult.

I tried what felt like a very clear and simple leadership strategy: I gathered the youth staff and decided to make following the sign-up deadlines mandatory. We just wouldn't allow any students who were late signing up to attend the event.

Needless to say, parents weren't thrilled with my decision. They were angry. I was being unfair. I was too rule-oriented. I was singling out their kids and making them an example. Oh, the phone calls I got! It wasn't a magical time in my ministry career.

But maybe it's not right to blame the parents.

No, wait—the church leadership team. It was *their* fault!

When I took on this new role, I jumped in with both feet. I gave it everything I had—my entire life, all of me. Forget the fact I already had another full-time job, a full load of classes, and a young family at home. Despite all that, I was ready to lead the entire ministry, including planning, administrating, counseling, and—most important in my mind—teaching the students. I felt the kids needed to hear from me. I thought it would be impossible to accomplish my goal of setting up the next youth pastor unless I had the microphone in my hand on Thursday nights. In my mind, a youth leader leads from the front. Our job is to speak from God's Word, imparting truth to hungry hearts.

But that wasn't what the church wanted from me. Shortly after I started leading, the pastor clued me in to his vision. I wasn't the one he wanted in front teaching the students each week.

I was hurt. My ego was shattered. How was I supposed to lead the group if I wasn't given the opportunity to be up front, visibly leading? I was expected to be responsible for the souls of the students in the room, and yet I was not the one actually getting to tend their souls. It didn't make any sense to me.

Hopefully you get it by now. Things were a real mess, with all kinds of emotional, spiritual, and relational baggage to sort through. There was probably enough blame to go around. And in the midst of the continuing crisis, I was forced to decide what kind of leader I was going to be. Would I be that guy who made the whole thing difficult for everyone at the church? Would I make the parents hate the ministry and force them to face themselves? Should I be the lightning rod for all the problems, make them my ministry identity, and become the failure the church needed so their new leader could come in as the savior of all ministry problems? Should I, for the sake of the egos of the youth staff, attack every critique?

It's safe to say I wasn't entirely sure what to do. There was no scapegoat, no one person or group to blame for the mess we were in. And the way out of the mess was equally unclear. I'm glad that, by the grace of God, I sought his plans before I relied on my own.

LEADING THE MINISTRY TO HOPE

I learned a lot about leading a youth ministry during those difficult months. As the summer stretched on, the volunteer team started to gel again, and students began to move through their anger. I was able to help the high school ministry leaders realize their best days were ahead. We started to gain traction in the hearts of the students, and a new relationship of trust and anticipation was born. As we continued to teach students more healthy habits, not only did things stabilize during our youth meetings, but also we started to gain control over things like the event registration problem.

Eventually we were able to stop focusing on the past and started looking forward to new and better things with the new person. As the rest of the summer progressed, students began to ask how they could pray for our ministry. More importantly they began to pray fervently that God would provide a new high school pastor they could follow and learn from.

That important time of emotional transition taught me a lot about ministry and what it takes to move through a time of crisis with hope for the future. After further reflection on those difficult days, I believe there are a number of things those of us in youth ministry need to do to allow God to use us to bring hope in a time of crisis.

Let students and parents know we care.

Recently I posted a story on my blog about a bad experience I'd had while buying an iMac. Within 24 hours I had dozens of comments from Apple advocates writing to defend the company. That's because Apple has a reputation for incredible customer service. Talk to any group of iPod or MacBook owners and you'll likely hear stories of how they went to the Apple Store because of some problem and had a brand-new product handed to them free of charge with no questions asked. As a result, Apple customers are tremendously loyal to the California-based company.

But Apple isn't alone. Starbucks also has legendary customer service. In *The Starbucks Experience*, Joseph Michelli documents how the emphasis on customer service begins with the company's top executives and trickles down to each store barista and eventually to their customers. All employees are trained to own this world-class customer service and express its principles in their own unique ways. At Starbucks, if a customer drops a drink in the store, they're never charged for a replacement. Instead, Starbucks turns a potentially embarrassing situation into a positive customer-service experience. And the result, again, is a global customer base that's incredibly loyal.

Reflecting on those businesses taught me I needed to ramp up our customer service. I needed to make sure our students and their parents felt valued by our ministry.

Think about it. Youth workers have dozens of opportunities to provide customer service. Every time we make a mistake, it's an opportunity to show students and their parents we care about their souls. As I thought about those companies, I realized customer service is really just about putting in the time and effort.

Suppose you have a ministry event that goes bad. Maybe the bus broke down at a rest stop and you allowed the students to get off the bus while you waited for a replacement. But in the midst of your impromptu game of ultimate Frisbee in the parking lot, a student ran in front of a moving car and broke a leg. And then you lost your temper and screamed at the whole group. Now parents are livid and your boss is getting angry calls about you. By the time you return to your office the next morning, there's a note on your door reading, "Meet me in my office at 8 a.m." You know that by 8 a.m., you'd better have a plan to deal with the problem. And that plan needs to include an effort to meet both the physical and emotional needs of the injured kid and ways the church can support the family. The effort and time we spend turning the problems we face into new opportunities to minister is totally worth it. But that can happen only if we own the problems. By being open and honest with your customer (and your boss), you'll communicate you're worth trusting, even when bad things happen.

Focusing on great "customer service" in ministry isn't just important in crisis situations. In fact, by consistently demonstrating you care, you'll solve some problems before they even come up. Little things like sending birthday cards, taking your volunteers out to recognize their service, and publicly praising students is a great way to build loyalty before there is a crisis.

Recognize how the ministry's story shapes people's feelings and emotions. At one point the most prevalent account of our ministry's story was a pretty ugly one. Our leader had been fired, the parents were angry, the youth staff was in conflict with the administration, and the whole ministry was in turmoil. Unfortunately there was at least some truth to all that. But that wasn't the whole story. If I'm in charge of the ministry, I'm also called to be in charge of the story of that ministry. It falls on us as leaders to define the identity of our ministries, to shape the way people see the past and the future. As we do that, we can lead those ministries to a healthier story.

Let's say the story being told about your ministry is: "It's lame." You hear it said in a bunch of different ways. The most obvious sign that this story has gained traction is that students aren't coming to your events. Your students would rather stay home and do homework than come over to your youth ministry center for an event. If the students won't come to your events because they're convinced algebra is more fun than your ministry, you can't disciple them.

Let's be honest: If the story of your ministry right now is the "it's lame" story, you're not going to be able to recast that overnight. But how do you begin to change it? You offer a different story, a more compelling one. Instead of trying to recast the story with an "it's a blast" spin, tell the "it's meaningful" story. Help students see that their lives are enhanced by coming to youth group. Pull them into the story that says "you matter" and "your soul is important." While they may not be convinced their time with you will be one big party, they may become convinced to identify with something that has more meaning.

Reshaping the story isn't as difficult as it might sound. You just have to consciously and consistently emphasize the story you want told. If the story you would like told is "it's meaningful," you'll need to find creative ways to emphasize that. In your communications with parents and students, demonstrate how what you're doing is meaningful. So maybe you publish a note you've received from a student about how a lesson impacted her. Retell that story at your next parents meeting, even if they've all heard it. When you're teaching at your weekly meeting, share your own story of how the lesson you're focusing on has impacted your own life. Encourage your students to write their own stories of how your meeting times are meaningful.

Seize the unique opportunities the crisis creates.
I have friends in youth ministry who seem to have been blessed with ministry-position gold mines. For every ounce of effort they put into their work, they seem to get an ounce of gold back.

This has never been the case for me.

From day one I've identified with Norman Dale's walk across the gym floor to meet that new group of students: "Let's see what kind of hand I've been dealt." Sometimes the hand God has dealt me has been wonderful, but more often it's presented challenges and problems. I chose one obvious situation to share with you, but there were plenty of others I could have written about. I've seen my share of crises—too many, to be honest.

There were many moments when I could've chosen to pack it in. I could've gone back to my adviser and chosen a new internship. I could've continued the status quo and allowed students to continue stepping on deadlines. I could've replaced the old volunteers with new ones. I could've whined about not getting to teach up front. I could've just tried to endure my time at the church, knowing I'd soon be gone and the situation would be someone else's problem. There were many times when I could have allowed the crisis to dictate success and failure. But I didn't. From the moment I had the meeting with the family pastor and took on the interim role, I saw this crisis as an opportunity to prepare the senior high youth group for their next pastor. Embracing the opportunity created room for success.

> CRISES ARE OPPORTUNITIES. THEY'RE CHANCES FOR US TO PROVE THAT WE CARE, THAT WE'RE LISTENING, AND THAT WE WANT TO DO SOMETHING TO ENCOURAGE THOSE AFFECTED.

Crises are opportunities. They're chances for us to prove that we care, that we're listening, and that we want to do something to encourage those affected. Every crisis gives us a new chance to offer emotional, spiritual, or even monetary support. Like the Good Samaritan of Jesus' parable, we can be the one who arrives at the scene prepared to spend whatever time, energy, or money is needed to address the problem. When we live in this way, we're communicating not only that we own the problems connected to our ministries, but that we passionately desire to correct them.

Norman Dale stepped into his own crisis—a hodgepodge of unteachable farm boys and angry parents—and turned them into the 1954 Indiana state basketball champs. But there was no film made about the team that lost the championship that year. No one remembers the coach of the South Bend Central basketball team, do they? They were the favored team—loaded with talent and expected to do great things. But they were unable to seize the opportunity that was theirs.

I think we're all drawn to stories like *Hoosiers* because we identify with them. We're the misfits, the ones who are hard to coach, and yet our leader and Savior takes us where we couldn't go ourselves. And then he asks us to share the challenge, to lead others to places they could never go themselves.

We can choose to view every challenge we face as an opportunity to express grace and love in a more powerful way. Our God is a God of second chances, restoration, forgiven mistakes, and circles of redemption. When you chose to embrace the toughest times as opportunities to point students to a life-changing relationship with Jesus, you're offering them the most powerful truth you could ever hope to teach.

CHAPTER 11

WHEN A TEEN
GETS PREGNANT

By Ginger Sinsabaugh MacDonald

IT WASN'T A TYPICAL NIGHT AT YOUTH GROUP. AFTER taking a hiatus from ministry to devote time to my new marriage, I'd been invited back to my old stomping grounds to speak on a chilly fall evening. The youth center hadn't changed, though the kids had. The same weird smell—a fusion of Doritos and dirty socks—lingered in the air. The foosball table still had a player that was held together with duct tape.

I spent the night catching up with kids who were now young adults. Jaime, who would always call "shotgun" on our trips, now had a car nicer than my own. Alvin, the kid who hacked into the church computer, now made his living fixing PCs. Jason, the joker who could put a piece of string into his nose and pull it out his mouth, was now serving in the military.

As we loaded up on junk food from the local 7-Eleven, we talked about what had changed and what hadn't, who was still around and who'd moved on, and the way the choices they'd made in junior high and high school continued to shape their lives as young adults—choices a lot more difficult than choosing a Slurpee flavor.

The conversation continued as we settled back in the youth center. I shouted out, "Okay, if you could rewind time and do things differently, what would you change?"

At first, I heard the expected.

"I would've finished school."

"I would've avoided the wrong crowd."

"I wouldn't have pulled the string through my nose."

But then there was the answer more painful than a brain freeze. "I wouldn't have had kids."

Oops! Did that really slip out of Marcie's mouth? Marcie, all of 20 years old, had not just one child, but two. Her first, Frankie, was born when Marcie was 15. The five-year-old had dark curly hair like his father, who sadly was not involved in Frankie's life. Marcie's second child, Zeek, was two years younger than his brother and was entering the age of ear infections and owies. Marcie and Zeek's father had married, but separated shortly after Zeek was born. Though she couldn't afford a divorce, Marcie insisted she could afford raising two children on her own without reliable financial support from either father. Meanwhile, Marcie's estranged husband had another baby on the way with someone else.

MARCIE LOOKED AT ME WITH EMBARRASSMENT, WISHING SHE COULD TAKE BACK HER WORDS. BUT LIKE TOOTHPASTE THAT'S BEEN SQUEEZED OUT OF THE TUBE, SHE COULDN'T.

Marcie looked at me with embarrassment, wishing she could take back her words. But like toothpaste that's been squeezed out of the tube, she couldn't.

"Does saying "I wish I didn't have kids" make me a bad person?"

I looked at Marcie, applauding her honesty, wondering how she managed to do it.

"No, Marcie. It makes you incredibly honest."

When you work in urban ministry, it seems teen pregnancy is as hard to avoid as potholes in the pavement. Though I've never owned my own diaper bag, during my 22 years of urban youth ministry I've felt the effects of 21 pregnancies among women under age 20. Twenty-one pregnancies that fast-forwarded these teens into real world responsibility—responsibility these young women weren't ready for. The pregnancies resulted in 18 births, two miscarriages, and one abortion, yet only two marriages.

Marcie's words took me back to a baby shower I'd attended years earlier for another young woman from a different church. I'd just gotten married and my husband accompanied me to the shower. This unwed mother was a pastor's kid; the baby's father was a vegan Muslim. The result was a very cute baby, but pretty lousy-tasting shower cake. The host of this shower, another member of my youth group, became a mom at age 15. The guests were faces I recognized from shaving-cream wars and pizza nights. But their carefree youth had been replaced by the 24/7 call of motherhood. There was Angelica, who dropped out of high school to take care of her infant. There was Daniela, the mom of two kids by different fathers and an expert at the "ins and outs" of collecting child support. Then there was Hanna, whom I hadn't seen since we got lost in the woods on a youth retreat. She had the rare combination of both a baby and a high school diploma. Hanna's older sister was also there, bragging she'd had her baby "late in the game"—at the ripe old age of 21. Heather couldn't make it, since her son was home with the flu.

While I enjoyed seeing their faces, I realized something was stranger than the tofu frosting. I was the only one there without a child—and the only one *with* a husband! With that realization, so many emotions flooded my mind that I didn't know what to say then, and I still have a hard time writing about it now. I was angry that none of my "hands off, pants on" talks seemed to have made a difference. I was confused about why marriage barely made a blip on their radar screens. But most of all, I was sick to my stomach that every single one of these young ladies had left church at a time when they needed God the most.

Of course, teen pregnancy isn't just an urban issue. It's in the burbs, in the small towns, even on Nickelodeon. According to the National Campaign to Prevent Teen Pregnancy, one out of three U.S. teenage girls gets pregnant before the age of 20. Teen pregnancy has become more and more accepted, with many high schools offering both birth control and baby care to students. So if the stork hasn't visited your youth group yet, he will before long. Hopefully you can glean insights from my experience on what to do and what not.

WHAT I'D CHANGE

As I think back on how I responded to the young women who became pregnant while they were part of my ministry, I've asked myself the same question I asked those former teens who used to meet in that funky-smelling youth room: *If I could rewind time and do things differently, what would I change?*

1. I'd recognize these girls weren't abandoning the church as much as the church was abandoning them.

As I watched an exodus of baby carriages leave church over the years, I believed the teen moms were abandoning the church. And part of me thought *good riddance.* I judged them, thinking their sin was dirtier than mine. Even though I had sexual sin in my closet, mine "didn't count" because it didn't result in a positive pregnancy test. I also felt very aware there were parents and other church members who believed teen pregnancy was reflecting poorly on the church: *If our youth department had leaders like the church down the street, we wouldn't be having this problem.* I started believing it too and became more concerned with the youth department's reputation than the girls who left the church.

That's when it hit me: These girls didn't abandon the church—the church abandoned them. After all the lessons telling kids to "choose life," the youth department—and the entire church—turned its back on the young women when they did make this choice. I wouldn't look the girls in the eye during their pregnancies for fear of blowing like a volcano. The church didn't offer programs to help them with this new stage of life. We gave little thought to how we might help these young moms finish high school and avoid the cycle of poverty single mothers so often face.

2. I would have a plan.

Looking back I realized the churches I served weren't pro-life; they were pro-fetus! And it wasn't so much out of judgment as it was out of lack of planning. Our youth department wasn't focused on meeting the needs of these teenage girls; we were focused on how the pregnancies affected us. Like other leaders in our ministry, I felt hurt, confused, and embarrassed. Had I let God down? Was I ineffective in youth ministry? Why did this happen to me?

I thought having a plan in place for dealing with teen pregnancy meant our youth staff was advocating promiscuity. Even as our leadership team was planning a "Purity for Sure-ity" series, we never discussed as a group what would happen if a girl got pregnant. We never asked ourselves a few hard questions: *Would she be allowed in youth group? How will this affect her future? How can a girl who can't pay for a week at camp pay for 18 years of child training?* By not answering these questions, we didn't know what to do when the inevitable happened.

3. I'd pay more attention to the reasons kids get pregnant.
I knew all about the birds and the bees, but I really didn't understand the dynamics of why so many teens *choose* to get pregnant. Yes, choose—regardless of whether statistics call these "unplanned pregnancies." Many teens believe a baby will be an answer to their current problems, not the birth of new concerns. "The baby will make him/her love me" or "I just want someone who will never leave me" are two common themes you'll hear from both teen moms *and* dads. When I started listening to kids' reasons for wanting to become a parent, they provided valuable insights on how to reach out to these young people before they end up teen parents. Here are some of the reasons teens get pregnant:

To have someone to love
To secure a relationship
To leave behind her own bad home situation and move somewhere else
To fit in with friends
To obtain an instant ticket to adulthood
To be like her mother, who was also a teen mom

When you keep in mind that young women (and young men) "just want someone to love," you'll approach your talks on "it's great to wait" differently. If a 14-year-old thinks getting pregnant is the best way to fast-forward her maturity, maybe you need a series on responsibility rather than one on self-control. If a teen desires to get pregnant to fit in with friends, talk about the strength of going against the flow. If any teens in your youth group are children of former teen parents, invite their moms to share about the dreams they had to put on hold to raise their children.

4. I wouldn't confuse the sin and the blessing.

In the midst of teen mama drama, it's easy to forget the psalmist's words: "Children are a blessing and a gift from the Lord" (Psalm 127:3, CEV). Like so many, I confused the blessin' with the messin'. The teenager who gets pregnant isn't the only one having sex—she's the one who gets caught. I found myself getting angry at the teen mother even though she chose life. Pointing fingers at the teen mother not only can shut down the lines of communication with us but also can intensify feelings of anger toward God. *Lots of kids are having sex!* she thinks. *How come I'm the one God let get pregnant?*

> EVEN THOUGH I'D TALKED ABOUT ABSTINENCE TILL I WAS BLUE IN THE FACE, I FELT RESPONSIBLE FOR HER ACTIONS. AND THOSE FEELINGS LIMITED MY ABILITY TO REACH OUT TO THE TEENAGE MOM WHEN SHE NEEDED ME.

5. I'd stay focused on the needs of the teenage mom rather than how the situation affected me.

When a teenager gets pregnant, regardless of the size, location, or denomination of the church, a few things are unavoidable. There will be angry confrontations with parents. The pastor will want a closed-door conversation. Some church members will be giving the stink eye on Sunday mornings. But I'm not just talking about what the pregnant teen experiences; that's what I've gone through as her youth pastor! I took the rap for her sin and I felt like a failure. Even though I'd talked about abstinence till I was blue in the face, I felt responsible for her actions.

And those feelings limited my ability to reach out to the teenage mom when she needed me.

That focus on my own experience also caused me to think of teen pregnancy as if it were a temporary issue, like botulism caused by bad potato salad at the church picnic. I acted as if once the girl had her baby, life would go back to normal. But the truth is: Although this particular pregnancy might affect me for only the next few months, it would shape the rest of this teenage mom's life. I minimized the degree to which that child would affect everything about her future, especially her education.

PLANNING FOR HOPE

The key to responding to teen pregnancy is having a plan in place. Looking back, I had a plan for just about everything else. What to do if there's a tornado. What to do if someone starts choking. What to do if a kid gets caught smoking on the camping trip. So now's your chance to do what I wish I'd done. The next time you meet with your senior pastor or church leadership team, discuss what the church will do when a teen gets pregnant. You need more than just a youth group plan—you need a church plan, a policy. If you don't know how to start the conversation, start by mentioning this:

One out of every three teen girls gets pregnant before the age of 20.
Two out of three of those will drop out of school.
Three out of three churches can help.

While there is no single right way to handle this issue, it must be handled. If the church is going to be vocal about choosing life, we'd better help the teen mom when she makes that choice. Your policy will be shaped by the size, demographics, and denomination of your congregation. A church with a big youth group and lots of two-parent households will have a different plan than a small church with mostly single parents. A charismatic church in the city will handle it differently than a conservative church in the country.

One thing is certain: You don't want to blow off this issue. God was big on helping the fatherless. He's the father of the fatherless (Psalm 68:5). In fact, there are more than 40 instances in the Hebrew Scriptures where God commands his people to take care of the *yothowm*, a word that means *destitute and orphaned*. *Destitute* could be the teen mom who's kicked out of her well-to-do suburban home yet receives no child support from the teen dad she met briefly on spring break. *Orphaned* could be the baby who's born fatherless or the multitude of teen parents (both male and female) who experience the pain of not knowing their own earthly fathers. However you look at these verses, teen parents and their children need our grace and love. So where do you start?

Here are two approaches a church might take in supporting teenage parents. The two options are not mutually exclusive:

Option A: Let the teen parent "stay a teen" in youth group.
While a teenage mom is a new parent, she's still a teen. Memories made in youth group are powerful and can continue to shape lives long after the lock-ins are over. They could very well be some of the best memories of a teenager's life. So some churches decide to support teenage parents by encouraging their continued full participation in youth group. If your church follows this path, you might want the teen mom (or dad) to step down from any leadership role he or she might have. For starters, the young parent will need more time to devote to new responsibilities. Besides that, keeping a teen mom/father as leader can send a mixed message: *If the church preaches "purity," is a teen parent the best choice for a leader?* But any change in the young parent's leadership role must be done out of love and concern, not out of condemnation, reminding the teen parent that he or she is still a vital part of the youth group.

Having a special evening where the group gathers to hear the teen mom share the real deal of her experience can be powerful. Ask a few tough questions: What is harder, being a teen parent or saying no to sex? How has the baby changed the dreams you had before the pregnancy?

I tend to think it's best if babies are kept out of the youth group meetings—unless it's an outreach program specifically designed for teen parents. After all, if 12-year-olds can't come to your high school youth group meetings, 12-month-olds shouldn't be allowed, either. Providing child care during youth meetings can be important in allowing teenage moms to participate fully.

Option B: Let the "big church" take the teenage parent under its wing. This alternate plan is simple: The teen mom made an adult decision, so now she has to live with the consequences. If your church decides on this plan, again, make sure it's explained to the teen parent with love and grace. Teenage parents shouldn't feel like they're "banned from youth activities," but instead should be given special attention to help them with their new responsibilities. This transition should be viewed as a passage of life, not a punishment.

Both Plans: Offer a Parenting Mentor.
In order to help a teenage mom in her new role in life, bless her with a mommy mentor. This mentor could be a former teen mom, a single mom, or a grandma with a big heart and open ears. A former teen parent can be especially effective as a mentor, since she's been through the experience and can offer hope and encouragement. This mentor could be sitting in your pews already. If not, contact a local crisis pregnancy center and brainstorm with them on the best ways to meet the new mom's need. Some congregations have older couples "adopt" the teen mom, becoming surrogate parents to her and her child. This can be extremely powerful if the teen parent came from a broken home.

As for the teen dad? Connect him with a mature Christian male in your congregation who experienced pain from not knowing his earthly father. This could encourage the teen dad to stay an active part of the child's life.

Be Her Ruth.

Teen pregnancy gives birth to all kinds of feelings, even if that pregnancy ends up in a miscarriage or abortion. So one of the most powerful things you can do is just listen. The pregnant teen needs a friend much more than she needs a lecture.

The biblical story of Ruth and Naomi points to the kind of friendship a teenage parent needs. Theirs was the ultimate story of friendship. Ruth stayed by Naomi's side, even though Naomi dealt with a lot of bad stuff—so much she changed her name to Mara, a name meaning "God has dealt bitterly with me." Ruth stuck by her side even though the situation got ugly. Be an encourager to the pregnant teen and stick by her when others don't. Now is the time when real ministry begins.

Don't Forget the Young Dads.

Statistics say 80 percent of the fathers of babies born to teen mothers don't marry the mother of their child. According to the National Campaign to Prevent Teen Pregnancy, these absent fathers pay an average of less than $800 annually for child support. If a teenage father is in your youth group, talk with him about his responsibilities and, equally important, his feelings. Many teen fathers are themselves children of an absent father and are simply continuing a cycle they were born into. So help the teen dad become the dad he wishes he'd had.

Start by talking to him about the relationship with his own father. What does he want to do the same way his dad did? What things will he do differently? You can dial things up a notch by having the teen dad write a letter to his father, no matter their relationship. (The letter does not have to actually be mailed.) This is a great way to work out the teen father's emotions.

You also have an opportunity to discuss the characteristics of God the Father. What makes a good father? How can a relationship with God through Christ help the teen dad with his responsibility? While Christ can't help the teen dad with child support, he can supply the encouragement a teen dad needs to finish high school and be a better provider financially. A relationship with Christ can also help the teen dad with self-control, guilt, anger, and the other emotions he may feel.

Adoption as an Option

Adoption sounds like the perfect and rational choice for teen moms. But in many low-income communities, adoption can be seen as a sign of weakness or selfishness. Rising to the occasion and dealing with whatever life throws you is considered a virtue. In *Promises I Can Keep: Why Poor Women Put Motherhood over Marriage*, Kathyrn Edin and Maria Kefalas point out:

> Whereas outsiders generally view childbearing in such circumstances as irresponsible and self destructive, within the social milieu of these down-and-out neighborhoods the norms work in reverse, and the choice to have a child despite the obstacles that lie ahead is a compelling demonstration of a young women's maturing and high moral stature.

So even if a well-meaning youth leader brings up adoption, it may be dismissed.

Hopefully that's not the case among the kids where you are. Adoption can be the ultimate act of love. Gina, a teen mom I interviewed, gave her child up for adoption. It wasn't a decision Gina made at the child's birth, but when her child was three. Gina came to the realization she couldn't do it all. As a single mom, she couldn't manage finishing school, working, and raising a child. Giving her child up for adoption was the toughest decision Gina ever made, but she knows her child now has parents who can do it all. They can give her son a future that she could not.

With today's open adoption laws, Gina can keep in touch with her son.

Many Christian adoption agencies, such as Bethany Christian Services, will assist pregnant teens in choosing an adoptive family and finding faith-based homes for babies. They also offer classes in parenting skills and support groups for teens who decide to take on the challenges of parenthood, helping them in the beginning as well as years down the road.

Before the Pregnancy and After—It's All about Education

There's a lot of good curriculum out there that encourages abstinence—from the "promise ring" approach to material that's loaded with graphic pictures of STDs sure to temporarily turn off the libido. Still, you might want to add a few other lessons into your program. Not lessons on birth control, but on self-control, goals, and self-esteem.

Ask teens where they want to be five years from now. What goals do they have? How would the responsibility of having a baby affect their ability to reach those goals? If any of your teens are children of former teen moms, have them ask their own moms about how becoming a parent shaped their pursuit of their own dreams. Do these moms desire their daughters or sons to be teen parents?

Be sure to challenge your teens by asking them how they would pay all the expenses that stem from raising a child. If teens are having trouble paying for their cell phones, have them think about what kind of allowance they'll need just to pay for diapers and baby formula. Always remind teens that while sex might feel good, reaching your goals and "getting your dream on" feels pretty good, too.

> TEEN MOMS ARE AT HIGH RISK OF DROPPING OUT OF SCHOOL AND, WITHOUT A HIGH-SCHOOL EDUCATION, THEY'RE LIKELY TO END UP IN THE CYCLE OF POVERTY. SO WORK ON PROGRAMS THAT ENCOURAGE TEEN PARENTS TO FINISH SCHOOL AND PROVIDE THE SUPPORT THAT CAN HELP THEM DO SO.

I'm not in favor of churches offering birth control education as a solution. Advocating birth control as an answer can keep teens stuck in the pain and emptiness of sexual activity instead of finding freedom and love in Christ.

But there's one form of birth control that has my approval: Sports. According to the Women's Sports Foundation, female athletes were less than half as likely to get pregnant as non-athletes (5 percent and

11 percent, respectively). On average, athletes had fewer sex partners, were more likely to be virgins, and tend to wait longer before their first sexual experience.

Teen moms are at high risk of dropping out of school and, without a high school education, they're likely to end up in the cycle of poverty. So work on programs that encourage teen parents to finish school, and provide the support that can help them do so. For example, offer babysitting so a young mom can study or get her a tutor when she falls behind. And be sure to celebrate when the teen parent graduates!

If a teen gets pregnant, it's not the end of the world—it's the beginning of a new one. Don't be disappointed with yourself; unless you gave the couple keys to the church van so they could "get busy" there, you probably did all you could. Yet a teenage pregnancy among your youth offers opportunities for real and lasting ministry. And it can allow you to extend your outreach to other teen moms in your community, partnering with schools or other area churches.

Teens can make amazing moms. I know of one named Mary who had a son named Jesus. I think she did a pretty good job.

CHAPTER 12

WHEN YOUR SPOUSE FEELS IGNORED

By Dale Kaufman

POWER. RAW, *WALKER, TEXAS RANGER*-KIND-OF POWER. That's what I had that weekend, and it was intoxicating—so intoxicating I forgot the most important person in my life other than Jesus.

I was a youth ministry veteran with nearly 13 years of experience serving as youth pastor of a great church in Colorado. I'd been given the opportunity to be the head of security for my denomination's regional youth conference, appropriately named Powersurge. The weekend conference was to be held in a four-star hotel in downtown Fort Worth, Texas, and was expected to draw around 500 junior high and high school students and adult leaders. It was my responsibility to help keep the participants safe, to corral any kids who dared try to sneak out of their rooms in the middle of the night, to protect the hotel property from the little hooligans, and to keep students from rushing the stage during the concerts.

I relished the assignment. I dreamed of saving some famous Christian musician who was being crushed by a crowd of adoring fans or of finding a poor, lost waif and returning him to his anguished youth worker as other youth pastors bowed down before me and declared, "We're not worthy! We're not worthy!"

So I prepared with reckless abandon. I assembled a team of people who would follow my every order without hesitation or question. (After all, lives could be at stake!) I scoured every inch of the place, even trying to check out the roof of the high-rise hotel in case some students got the bright idea to bungee-jump off the top of the building. I had it all covered, and I waited in eager expectation for the weekend to arrive.

By the way, did I mention I was a newlywed? Sorry, I think I forgot that part amid all the excitement of reliving this ministry opportunity where I would be a hero to hundreds of students!

Oh, yes, I was married—married for six months to a beautiful woman who had a vision of doing ministry alongside me. The trouble was, Pam was less experienced in ministry than I was. When we met, she was a volunteer youth worker at a different church (different denomination) than mine. During our dating and engagement period, she made the transition to my church and, after our wedding, threw herself into doing ministry alongside me. Which was great, except for one thing: Due to her lack of experience, I felt she needed several years of "training" to get to the ministry level I'd already "attained." So it became very easy for me to treat my new bride as more of a ministry slave than a ministry equal. I didn't mean to, but having done youth ministry for so long, I had developed a great deal of pride—er, I mean, a strong sense of how things needed to be done.

Just five months into our marriage (and only a few weeks before the big conference), my wife was mischievously chasing a young student through the church in a vain attempt to defend my honor. (The girl had made fun of my bald head!) Pam missed the steps at the entryway of the church and fell, landing on her knee—which promptly broke in two, requiring a trip to the emergency room and knee surgery on Thanksgiving Day! To be honest, this irritated me. Here I was, trying to hold my ministry together and get ready for this big event, and now I had to take care of my wife while she healed up!

By the time of the Powersurge event in December, Pam was still in a full leg brace and on crutches, not particularly ready to walk around a Texas hotel all day as a member of my security team. Since she was semi-immobile, we (and by "we" I mean "I") decided the best way she could help at Powersurge was to be a chaperone for some of our youth group's senior high girls. That way she could take part in the experience but wouldn't have to walk as much. We'd be able to see each other in passing, and I could concentrate on my power-tripping security job. She could help out the other chaperones on the 8-hour drive in the church van with the students. (I couldn't help with that because it was imperative I be there early to get things in place, so I drove down the day before with my student assistant.)

By this time, I'm sure you're amazed at what a thoughtful, considerate husband I was! But wait, there's more.

The event began as planned, and the rest of my security team and I kept busy as rent-a-cops. It was a lot of fun, and being in charge of the whole deal was a great ego-stroker for me. The students from our youth group were having a good time, and I hardly noticed my wife seemed a bit distant from me as the weekend progressed. (Imagine that!) Then, on the second full day of the event, she slipped while getting into the bathtub in her room, wrenching her knee and falling into the tub. It took three girls to help her get out of the tub.

When I heard about what had happened, I did what any good youth ministry husband would do. I asked: "Are you okay to finish out the weekend? Because there really aren't any other female counselors available."

Needless to say, the air got decidedly cooler in the hallway where we were talking!

At the end of Powersurge, as the youth group members were piling into the vans to head back to Colorado, I pulled the most boneheaded move of all. My wife was standing in the hotel entrance, in terrible pain, her eyes brimming with tears. She'd been scheduled to go home with the students, but I still had responsibilities to the event and wouldn't be heading home for several more hours. Pam pleaded with me to let her wait and drive home with me. But all I could think of was how I wanted her to ride back in the van and take care of the students! So you guessed it: I made her get in the van and waved as she rode off, blissfully unaware of the horrible thing I'd just made her do.

Of course, I had no idea I was sending her into a dangerous Texas ice storm that would turn the 8-hour trip into an 18-hour nightmare of icy roads and gale-force winds. But that's beside the point. I was concerned only about the students, and I totally ignored my wife's needs. I'd forgotten that God calls us to place our spouses above others, and that our ministries and our prayers are hindered when we get our priorities out of balance.

After I watched the van pull away, as I turned and walked back into the hotel, my arm was grabbed forcefully by another pastor at the event, a woman I deeply respect. She pulled me over to a chair and said, "Sit down, Dale," in a tone that let me know I'd messed up. She'd watched the scene at the hotel door, and she'd seen the anguish in my wife's eyes that I'd ignored. For the next hour, she laid into me, raking me over the coals for ignoring my beautiful wife and causing terrible damage to my marriage and to my witness.

During that hour, I had my priorities shifted like never before. My sin was laid bare, and I dissolved into tears—a very rare occurrence for me! I saw what an idiot I'd been, putting my ministry ahead of my marriage. I realized my pride had led me to dishonor not just my wife, but God as well. I'd shown utter insensitivity to the needs of this woman I'd promised less than a year before to love, honor, and cherish for the rest of our life together. I don't remember everything that pastor said, but I do remember weeping over my sin and promising to God that I would do whatever I could to make it up to my wife. (Assuming she was still there when I got back—I couldn't have blamed her if she'd decided to pack up her things and move back home to Mother!)

I learned more from that experience about how God wants us to treat our spouses than any other time in my life. They're lessons that all of us who do ministry—especially youth ministry—need to take to heart.

LEARNING MY LESSONS

My pride and need for control got in the way of ministering to my wife. Even though I was in a "ministry mode," that was no excuse for ignoring her. In fact, by ignoring Pam, I was sending a message to both my students and the other adult leaders that ministry should come before marriage. Even though I didn't realize it until later, my wife—the woman I'd promised to love and cherish "till death do us part"—had been demeaned and made to feel less important to me than a teenager who would only be in my life for a short time.

Lesson 1: Your spouse is your number one ministry, not your students!

Let's face it: Youth ministry is an extremely demanding profession. Kids typically have no concept of what it means to be married. All they know is they have a crisis, and they want their youth pastor to be there for them. So it is very easy for them to push through boundaries in order to get to you. Between their demands, the demands of parents and other church people,

> BY IGNORING PAM, I WAS SENDING A MESSAGE TO BOTH MY STUDENTS AND THE OTHER ADULT LEADERS THAT MINISTRY SHOULD COME BEFORE MARRIAGE.

and what the senior pastor expects of us, it's very easy to shove aside our spouses, figuring they love us and want us to be successful in ministry. We figure if they married a youth pastor, they ought to take what "comes with the job."

But your spouse didn't marry the church or your youth group. Your spouse married you—and you married him or her! And God calls you first and foremost to minister to and meet the needs of your spouse—before you meet the needs of the church. Sure, there are emergency times when a crisis occurs and you need to elevate church ministry to number one status temporarily. But the key word here is *temporarily*. Your spouse needs to know that he or she comes before your ministry, that he or she is the most important person to you outside of Jesus, and that when you said that wedding vow about honoring that person above all others, you really meant it.

Words get cheap here, by the way. It's very easy to tell your wife she is important, to tell your husband you value him above all others, and then turn around and ignore that person when the demands of ministry get intense. If you're forever giving up time with your spouse in order to minister to your students, it doesn't matter what wonderful praise you lay on your wife or husband when you return. It's going to feel flat and meaningless.

Lesson 2: The fact that your spouse is involved in the same ministry you are doesn't give you permission to ignore him or her.

Because my wife and I were doing the "same ministry" that weekend, I thought I was justified in not paying the kind of attention to her I should have. I figured we were doing ministry "together"—so she shouldn't have felt ignored. I thought she was getting the same kind of fulfillment from the weekend that I was. I couldn't have been more wrong! I needed to remember that, while she was just as committed to the kids as I was, her needs for support and love and intimacy from me didn't disappear at the hotel door. (And because she was injured, her needs were even greater, which made my lack of compassion all the more egregious.)

Lesson 3: God doesn't bless your secondary ministry (youth ministry) if you don't give priority to your first ministry (your spouse).

This was a hard lesson for me to learn. When I do youth ministry, I'm *driven*. When a special event or activity is approaching—or even just a normal youth group meeting (if there is such a thing)—I go into what my family now refers to as "ministry mode." I get intensely focused on what's coming up, and my mind is occupied with an assortment of tasks that need to get done and people who will need an extra touch of ministry from me. My guess is you're probably much the same. It's a big part of what makes us good youth workers. We're passionate and devoted to the people God has called us to minister to.

But if you're married, your first ministry is to your spouse—and to your children. If we neglect our first ministry, no matter how many students we have in our youth groups, no matter how many accolades we get from parents or church leaders, no matter how many national conferences we get invited to attend and present the keynote speech—it will all be in vain. Such work is worthless in the final judgment if we lose our spouses or our children because we've ignored their needs. And remember this: 1 Peter 3:7 says if you don't honor your spouse and meet his or her needs, your prayers are hindered. In other words, ignore your spouse and you may find

God ignoring your prayers! That's not something any of us ought to be taking chances with!

Lesson 4: You aren't God's answer to youth ministry, but you are God's answer to the needs of your spouse.
I had to learn I'm not indispensable to God getting his work done in the world. Neither are you. Get off the ministry power trip. Lay your pride aside. 'Nuff said.

Although I'm not God's answer to youth ministry, I'm God's answer to my wife's needs! God has called me first and foremost to do ministry with and to my wife. No one can do it better than I can. I'm called to lay aside myself in order to minister to and love my wife. The Bible says a husband is supposed to love his wife as Christ loves the church— enough to die for her. If that's not a great power trip, I don't know what is! The privilege I have to care for, to love, to sacrifice for, and to edify my wife is the highest privilege and responsibility I will ever have.

When I get that kind of perspective, it makes it much easier to shift my focus to the right kind of power trip—the kind that will help build up my family and will also pay big dividends in ministry. For instance, on that Powersurge weekend, if I'd ministered to my wife in the way I should have, it would have spoken volumes to the students. Seeing their youth pastor love his wife sacrificially would say a lot more to students than a 10-minute youth talk. Of course, you don't love your spouse sacrificially just to teach a lesson to your students. You do it because that's what love does!

FINDING HOPE
Obviously I should have paid more attention to my wife and listened to her real needs. This sounds so simple after the fact. At the time I was completely absorbed in what I was doing and in making sure my ministry responsibilities were carried out well. And because I was so absorbed, I didn't take the time to consider how my wife was feeling, what she was struggling with, or how I could help her. I shoved her aside in my mind, paying attention to what I thought was a greater

need. Had I stopped even once that weekend and really paid attention to what she was saying and what she needed, the weekend would have ended much differently for us!

I'm ashamed to say it, but my wife was somewhere down my list of priorities that weekend, and so it became tremendously easy to ignore her—even when she was in serious pain! She should have been in first place. Because she wasn't, it took a long time for us to work through the pain I had inflicted on her. I repented (to her and to God), she forgave me, and eventually I got out of the proverbial doghouse—but it's a doghouse I never want to see the inside of again!

Maybe you're seeing a painful reflection of yourself in my story. If so, I want to offer you some wonderful hope: You can change! If you've ignored your spouse in favor of your ministry, repent and ask for her or his forgiveness, as well as God's. Commit before God and your spouse that you will put the one you married before your ministry, then follow up your words with actions—that's the really fun part!

If you've been ignoring your spouse, do an about-face: Spend time actively loving your spouse. (I've found *The Five Love Languages* by Gary Chapman to be an excellent way to understand how your spouse feels and communicates love). Let a staff member or volunteer lead that junior high Bible study—and then take your spouse out for dinner instead! Rekindle the romance and passion in your marriage. Pray for and with your spouse. Meet his or her needs for emotional, spiritual, physical, and sexual intimacy. Become a student of your wife or your husband. Learn all you can, and practice what you learn every day of your life together!

In the end, you'll find your marriage has more strength, your ministry has more credibility, your prayers have more influence, and your life will have more power than Walker, Texas Ranger, could ever dream of having!

CHAPTER 13

WHEN TRAGEDY STRIKES YOUR MINISTRY
By Pete Brokopp

I SAT AT A TABLE IN A MAKESHIFT RESTAURANT WITH A TIN ROOF supported by poles. I ordered a Coke and then closed my eyes, my head in my hands. I noticed I was shaking. Was it because I'd had nothing to eat or drink all day, or was it the events of the last 16 hours?

Ten years earlier, I'd come to Burkina Faso as a missionary. One of my main goals was to set up a program that would offer valuable mission experiences for youth groups in U.S. churches. I also helped take care of field business and hosted mission teams and short-term missionaries. I loved my ministry! But I'd just been though perhaps the most challenging experience of my entire time in Burkina Faso.

Just the previous evening, our missionary team had met with two executives from our U.S. headquarters, sharing and praying with them. The evening started on a light note with a few funny stories exchanged. We'd just served ourselves some strawberry pie when Ann, a young woman who'd come on a four-month, short-term mission trip, said she wasn't feeling well. Rather than interrupt the meeting to have someone take her home, she decided to lie down and rest. We commented after she left the room about what a good addition she was to our team, how she'd helped us in various areas, and what an encouragement she was to us. Then we continued our meeting.

Ann never appeared again during our meeting, so when we were finished, we asked her to come out so we could pray with her. Since she still wasn't feeling well, one of our missionaries took the initiative to call a missionary doctor who lived nearby. He came over quickly and checked her vitals. Though he didn't find anything wrong, he scheduled her for an EKG the next morning just to make sure nothing was going on.

We were all getting ready to leave for the night when Ann made the comment, "Well, in any case, no matter what happens, I know where I'm going." Since no one likes to be alone when they're sick, she decided to spend the night with another missionary who had been mentoring her and working closely with her throughout her stay.

Early the next morning, our house phone rang. The voice on the other end was desperate: "Please pray for Ann. She's not breathing."

Not breathing? Surely the caller meant Ann was having difficulty breathing. Had she eaten something bad the night before? Was she having some kind of anaphylactic shock? My wife and I prayed that the Lord would restore her breath. Then my cell phone rang and another voice desperately screamed, "Get over here! Now!"

I threw on my clothes and rushed over to the house where Ann had spent the night. Her mentor, Laura, met me at the door, saying, "Pete, I think she's gone." In the room where Ann had slept, the doctor was performing CPR on her with tears streaming down his face. His breath wheezed as he was working so hard, intent on keeping Ann alive. My missionary team leader was crying out to God, and he admonished me to pray, so I did. Suddenly, I felt as if someone had patted me on the shoulder and released me from praying.

I looked at Ann. She was no longer there.

The realization that Ann had died took a while to set in. But once it did, the horrifying question hit, "What do I do now?" My thoughts were jumbled and I was unable to think straight. At first I didn't even feel clearheaded enough to pray and ask God for wisdom. Then the fog dissipated, and I realized I needed to help my colleagues deal with Ann's death. I took Laura out to the living room and called an ambulance.

Finally, after more than a half hour of CPR, the doctor stopped and declared her deceased; then the ambulance finally arrived. We called the U.S. Embassy and the staff there were amazing! Although they'd never had to deal with an American citizen's death in the country, they dug up the protocol and walked us through it—giving us advice, supporting us, and helping us through the paperwork until Ann's body left the country. We discovered that Ann had mentioned she'd purchased some insurance to cover her evacuation from the country if she got sick and needed hospitalization or if she died. Wow! She'd even told another member of our team where the insurance card was.

I knew the hardest step in the process would be contacting Ann's parents. She'd been their only child, the apple of their eye, the darling of her home church and the small rural community surrounding it. Her father had been apprehensive of her trip to Burkina and would surely take the news hard. Even though it was just 3 a.m. back in the United States, we decided to call Ann's home pastor to get his advice on what we should do. Amazingly, we got a great connection, and the pastor decided it would be best if he contacted the family himself.

The U.S. Embassy staff called Ann's insurance company and also learned there was only one full-service funeral home in the country. (Most people in Burkina Faso bury their dead quickly before their bodies begin to decompose.) The next big issue was the autopsy. Would one be required by the U.S. government? The airline? The Burkinabe government? The insurance company? Ann's family? We couldn't move Ann's body until we had an answer to this question. But we were having a difficult time reaching the pastor we'd contacted. And we knew it would be even more devastating for the family to receive the news from someone at the U.S. Embassy rather than from their pastor.

Finally we were able to get the morgue to agree to accept Ann's body even though we couldn't yet declare whether an autopsy was needed. It was a tough job, as they wanted to embalm her. Finally we were able to get through to the pastor and the family, and heard that no one needed an autopsy. It was pretty apparent she'd passed away from either a heart attack or a heart aneurysm.

Our next step was choosing a casket. We wanted to honor Ann and her family by choosing a nice one. The best one we found was made out of varnished plywood. I secured it and the morgue finished its business.

With that issue settled, I finally made my way across the street to the tin-roofed restaurant for that Coke break at the makeshift bar. As I sat there, the questions ran through my mind: *How could this happen? Where is God in all this?* This young woman had come to this poverty-plagued country hoping to make a difference. She was an only child. How could God seemingly overlook her parents' sacrifice? Why would he take the life of someone who was doing important kingdom work, sharing the gospel in this poor country where hope often seems so hard to find?

> THE QUESTIONS RAN THROUGH MY MIND: HOW COULD THIS HAPPEN? WHERE IS GOD IN ALL THIS?

WHAT DID WE DO WRONG?

What should we have done differently? That's a critical question to ask any time some part of our ministry fails. As we look back on times when things haven't gone as we'd hoped or planned, there are almost always things we can learn, things we could have done better. In our case—

1. We should have required medical and evacuation insurance for each team member and short-termer.

The Lord took care of us and prompted Ann to secure insurance on her own before the trip. But imagine how difficult and expensive it would have been if Ann hadn't had that insurance! Now we require insurance for everyone coming out.

2. We took life for granted.

Shortly after the doctor declared Ann's death, he looked at me and said, "Pete, I just don't understand—I've seen you sicker than that three times in this year alone." And he was right: I'd been too close to a gunfire exchange, someone had tried to stab me, I'd been hospitalized twice, and I'd had to return to the United States for a time because of a blockage in my gall system. In our work here, we've often walked through the valley of the shadow of death and experienced God's protection. But that should never lead us to take life for granted.

Most of the time we can look at our ministry failures and learn from them. But there are also times when things just happen. Sometimes bad things happen to good people, no matter what we do. Sometimes God allows things to happen that don't make sense to us, and we have to trust that he will use them for our good and his glory.

> IN OUR WORK HERE, WE'VE OFTEN WALKED THROUGH THE VALLEY OF THE SHADOW OF DEATH AND EXPERIENCED GOD'S PROTECTION. BUT THAT SHOULD NEVER LEAD US TO TAKE LIFE FOR GRANTED.

It turns out that Ann had experienced chest pains many times in the past. She'd never had them checked out and apparently nothing ever showed up on any physical exam she'd had. Back in the United States, she lived in a rural area 45 minutes from the closest trauma center. She was actually better off in Burkina Faso, where our doctor lived just two minutes away. The doctor had checked her out (even though she didn't even want to see a doctor), and her initial symptoms didn't seem severe. We'd even made appointments for further tests, just to make sure. In short, there was absolutely nothing related to her medical care that we could have done differently.

The reality is Ann could have had the same attack in North America and the results would almost certainly have been the same. I know in my head we didn't do anything wrong. But somehow I find my heart questioning it. I feel guilty.

3. We failed to count the cost.

In our years working in Burkina Faso, we'd hosted hundreds of short-term missionaries and individuals on teams, and we'd never even had to send one home early for being sick or injured. So when this happened, I didn't want the news to escape because I thought the story would be exaggerated, that short-termers would be afraid to leave the "safety" of America. The reality is that, given all the precautions we take and all the organizing work that paves the way for the teams who come here, their time serving with us may well be safer than if they'd attended a summer camp back in North America. But I was worried people would be reluctant to serve with our ministry if they heard about Ann's death.

But over time I've realized the importance of both short- and long-term team members counting the cost. I've decided I'm looking for short-termers who *are* willing to lay their entire lives on the line for Christ, people who *are* completely sold out and committed. People go on mission trips for many different reasons: To experience a different country and culture; to deepen their own faith; to participate in a significant ministry; to see if missions is something God would have them do in the future. Some of these are good reasons; others aren't. I've decided my own goal for the short-termers who serve with us isn't about how much they can accomplish or how much money they can raise to advance their ministry, but rather that God do a great work in their lives. It's when kids come out to the mission field willing to offer everything to God that God is freed to work amazing things in their lives.

> IT'S WHEN KIDS COME OUT TO THE MISSION FIELD WILLING TO OFFER EVERYTHING TO GOD THAT GOD IS FREED TO WORK AMAZING THINGS IN THEIR LIVES.

CHANGING PERSPECTIVE, FINDING HOPE

As I sat at that restaurant table that day, the familiar words from 2 Corinthians 12:9 came to mind: "My grace is sufficient for you." At that point I wasn't sure I felt that way. This was one of the hardest times I'd gone through. It was one of the worst days of my life. But as I've reflected further, I've come to realize God's grace really *is* always sufficient—that day and every day. It's just that we sometimes need a shift in perspective to fully experience that grace. I believe that shift involves three things:

First, we open ourselves to grace as we learn to view things from the perspective of eternity.
Our struggles here on Earth pale in comparison with the greatness of living in heaven with our Creator and in the presence of our Lord and Savior Jesus Christ. Earthly trials become insignificant when we consider the absence of tears, sickness, pain, death, and sin, forever and ever. Any suffering here on Earth, no matter how great or small, will pass, eventually. Even if the pain does last a lifetime on Earth, it is short when compared with eternity. So as youth leaders, our hope is found when we change our perspective to that of eternity and the greatness of God. Earthly difficulties will pass, but through God's grace we will live out eternity in extreme blessing.

Second, we open ourselves to grace as we learn to view all that happens in light of our heavenly Father's love.
Sometimes it's hard for us to understand how the caring God who loves us so much can allow difficult events that cause us such pain and hurt. Yet in every situation we can see evidence of God's love. When I sat there asking, "Where are you, God?" God showed me numerous examples of how his love had shown through in this terrible situation. For example:

That morning, the different members of our missionary team all experienced God powerfully present in different ways.

God inspired Ann to purchase the insurance that made it much easier for us to care for her body appropriately and to know we were following her desire in the way it was handled.

He put people in the Embassy who went beyond what they needed to do to help us.

He allowed us to "go overboard" in calling a doctor the night before, even though Ann didn't want us to call, and we usually wouldn't call a doctor for what appears to be stomach pain or bad heartburn! But that gave us a sense of assurance we had done everything we could have possibly done.

Ann came from a good church with a good pastor, who in the midst of a hard time did his best to be an encouragement for us.

God helped our missionary team develop the kind of close relationships that allowed us to bear one another's burdens during this time of crisis.

Finally, we open ourselves to grace as we realize that sometimes God brings successes not just in spite of our trials and failures, but also sometimes because of them.
Throughout my time as a youth pastor and then as a missionary, the possibility someone might die while in my care was always my greatest fear. I could deal with kids doing bad things; I could deal with people who couldn't get along; I could deal with not accomplishing the mission. I could even deal with a moral failure. But death? Incomprehensible!

But the seeds of the gospel and the growth of the church are often watered with the blood of saints. The mission trip in which Ann participated was not a failure. It was, in fact, probably one of the most successful mission trips to Burkina I've ever been part of. And in many ways the trip was a success because of her death. For example:

Ann died on a Wednesday, a day she usually taught an evening class for people learning English as a second language. Since we were still all in shock and mourning, we sent someone to cancel the class that night. In the process of telling the students what had happened, the person shared the gospel, mentioning Ann's words of assurance that she'd be in heaven should she die. Thirty students were in the class, most of whom were Muslim. Two of those students accepted Christ shortly thereafter, and one of them has already led five others to Christ!

Ann's death brought a renewed commitment to reaching lives for Christ among the leaders of the local Burkinabe church. It has also helped to motivate the youth to completely restructure their youth center and programming to be more effective in reaching the lost.

We've seen an influx of people who want to take Ann's place on the field.

Our organization held its regional leadership conferences within a few days of Ann's death. I believe her story significantly touched every leader there and renewed the organization's commitment to short-term missions.

Her death brought our team of missionaries closer together.

Only eternity will show the full, long-term magnitude of Ann's sacrifice. But it's clear to me that this tragedy led to some of the greatest successes we've ever experienced in short-term ministry in Burkina Faso. And this is so often true—God takes things that look like failures and uses them to bring about revival or great developments for his church. I think about Joseph's personal tragedy in Genesis 37-39, during which he is thrown into a well, sold as a slave, and later imprisoned for something he didn't do. But God uses these events to place Joseph in a position of power in a foreign land and brings his extended family into that land where they grow into a nation.

> GOD TAKES THINGS THAT LOOK LIKE FAILURES AND USES THEM TO BRING ABOUT REVIVAL OR GREAT DEVELOPMENTS FOR HIS CHURCH.

When we experience failure, struggle, or tragedy in our ministries, we still need to ask ourselves what we could have done differently and learn from mistakes we've made. But when there's nothing we could have changed, we need not lose hope. We can still learn from the experience. We can seek to view our situation from God's perspective of eternity. We can find the signs of God's love amid the difficulties. And we can look for the ways God brings success even when all we can see is failure.

We recently welcomed a work team who had traveled here to help us build an addition on a youth center. They were so excited about the project, but soon after arriving, one by one, they began to fall ill with some vicious bug they'd brought with them from the States. It was hot, they were miserable, and some of them barely got to see the worksite the whole time they were here. What a waste, right? Not at all! The main comment they had as they prepared to return home was, "Now we know what you experience when you have so much work to do. Now we know better how to pray for you and other missionaries."

The people who went on that trip could have seen it as a huge failure, thinking all the work and money they'd put into making that trip had been for nothing. But the members saw God's perspective of eternity: They knew they would get better eventually, and they knew their mission trip's importance went deeper than what was "accomplished" to the spiritual lessons learned and the attitudes displayed. They praised God that the member of their team who couldn't afford to fall ill because of his job situation at home was able to stay healthy and could offer care to the others. And their trip was successful because of the trials: They returned with a more intimate understanding of the struggles missionaries face in the field. They returned knowing how to pray for missionaries and how to get others to pray. That mission trip was a great success—despite its failures. It's wonderful to know God's grace is always ready for us, to accept us when it's time for us to enter his presence, and to help us learn from the death of a servant.

CHAPTER 14

WHEN YOU FAIL MORALLY
By Mary Huebner

HIS SCREEN NAME POPPED UP ON MY "BUDDY LIST" on my laptop. I felt that eyes-roll-back-in-your-head involuntary adrenaline rush that's so very addicting.

He IMed me. My heartbeat quickened. I'd known him for years: He'd been a student at a senior high camp I'd directed years ago, then worked as an admissions representative for one of our church colleges, and now was a youth pastor. He was many years my junior, but an adult. He lived five states away, and we rarely saw each other in person. His words flashed up on my screen:

Hey Baby.

I responded: Hey Baby.

Where are you? Why are you up so late?

Different time zone. I'm in New Orleans—painted the town red tonight. ;)

Oh really? ;)

Yeah, I LOVE this city, don't know why people are so scared of it. Although, there IS an underlying sensuality to it. I even unbuttoned my blouse an extra button walking the streets tonight. What was that about? I never do that.

Why do you think you did that?

Don't know, really. Maybe it was the hurricane I drank.

Maybe. :)

OK, I should hit the sack. We r sight-seeing tomorrow. Sweet dreams, Baby.

Do you ever dream about "us"?

From there, the conversation grew more intimate. The adrenaline escalated. There was no "Internet sex," but the mood progressed from affectionate to more sexual.

When I finally signed off, I felt numb. I clicked the IM window shut and it was all gone—lost in cyberspace. It all seemed very surreal. It was very late. I crawled into bed and prayed, "God, I have lost my mind. I love my husband. How did that just happen?"

When I woke up the next morning, it all seemed like a distant dream. I vowed in my head and heart never to chat with anyone online again—ever!

Over the next few months I broke my vow and chatted with him several more times. I thought we could handle having friendly conversations about our lives without innuendo. But each time we chatted, we ended up back at the same place. I would make another vow only to break it when he signed on again. I was addicted. My spiritual formation didn't eliminate my raging emotional need or the rush I got from the experience.

It didn't take long for the relationship between us to begin to deteriorate. When I tried to end the inappropriate conversation, his tone shifted. I soon felt he was IMing me out of obligation, like I was excess baggage he was ready to be done with.

The relationship rotted—and true to the Word, it died. Sin is death. It may be tempting, it may be intoxicating, it may offer us a fun time or an adrenaline rush—but in the end, sin is *most surely* death.

On a Sunday morning a few months later, I learned this man had confessed to having an affair with another married woman. The Holy Spirit used that revelation to knock me onto my knees and into my senses. I couldn't carry my shame or the fear of being found out one more moment. I went to my husband, Denny, who's also the senior pastor of our church. I confessed my unfaithfulness to him.

"That could have been me," I said. "I'm so very sorry."

In that moment my husband and I began the emotional journey back to each other.

Fast-forward five months later.

Denny got a call from the state pastor of our denomination

asking both of us to meet him for lunch. We made a few guesses, but neither of us knew the reason he wanted to see us.

The state pastor was waiting for us when we pulled into the parking lot of the Italian restaurant where we'd agreed to meet. He held the door for us as we entered the restaurant, and we were seated in a booth. After the waitress took our order, the state pastor told us an anecdote about getting kicked out of the park when he was a child. I served everyone the salad from the bowl on the table.

Then the bomb was dropped.

"Mary, you've been accused of some very serious things. Have you had an inappropriate relationship with someone?" the state pastor asked.

I dropped my fork.

Before I could say anything, Denny spoke up: "Look, I don't know what you've heard, but you don't know the whole story."

The state pastor said, "No, Denny, *you* don't understand. Your wife is a sexual predator."

Sexual predator.

The words hung in the air.

> I COULD FEEL THE LIFE BEING SUCKED OUT OF ME.

"Mary, you have a choice to make," the state pastor said. "Either you can confess right now and step into the restoration process with the credentials committee of the state—or we can launch a full investigation."

I could feel the life being sucked out of me; I was broken. *What if I hadn't confessed to Denny? What if he didn't know anything about this? What do these people think I've done? Is my ministry over for good?*

I nodded in response to his demands. I knew I wasn't a predator, but I also knew I was guilty of sin. And I knew the nuances of what had actually happened wouldn't matter at the end of the day. I was getting kicked out of the park.

"Look, regardless of what I have done or what you think I have done, and even though the other person is *not* a minor, I'll do whatever you ask," I told him. "Treat me as if I *were* a sexual predator. I want to do the restoration process by the letter of the law so there is no question of my integrity or Denny's integrity when the process is complete."

This was the absolute *worst* thing I could *ever* have imagined happening to me. I was a state and national youth leader in a holiness denomination/movement, and now my sin—sin I wasn't supposed to have since I was sanctified—was being made public. I was asked to confess my sin to everyone I'd ever worked for or with. I felt like all the good work I'd done over my many years in ministry was now being questioned.

Although I knew the restoration process would be agonizing, I really expected to receive grace from the people I'd worked with most closely, those who knew me well. For the most part, I was wrong. A working relationship, even in ministry (or maybe especially in ministry), does not always equal true community.

I was subjected to a conference call where those I'd worked with fired their best shots at me:

"How could you do this to *me*?"

"Have you thought of the thousands of youth you've let down and how destroyed they will be—how you have ruined their lives?"

"Do you realize that statistics show that your own sons will act out and hit rock bottom in three years due to your failure?"

"Do you realize you're the first female in our denomination to have a moral failure?"

"We have pulled all the curriculum you've written off the presses!"

But not every response was like that. There were also points of great light in which people rose to the occasion and imparted grace and healing to my wounded and sin-sick soul:

"Mary, this is exactly why Christ died. He placed your sin in the sea of forgetfulness and posted a sign that says 'NO FISHIN!'"

"The national leaders of the church wanted me to kick you off my team, but I'm not going to. I want you to stay as a consultant while you're in the restoration process. I want to walk through this with you."

"Mary, we will not let you step down from your position. We will come alongside you and journey with you. We all deal with sin—yours is just out there on the table at the moment and that probably makes you more healthy than the rest of us."

"We have all been to some dark places, Mary. The fact that you've been to a dark place, then repented, and are in the restoration process qualifies you for real ministry in my opinion."

Over time I came to realize that what seemed like the absolute worst thing that could ever happen to me was actually a *good* thing—a time during which I experienced God's grace in a profound way. God provided the grace I needed to deal with my emotional need. There is incredible freedom in having your sin discovered—even if that freedom isn't immediate. It settles the issue of confession and allows you to move on and deal with the business of being real before God and allowing him to meet you—all of you—right where you are and begin to heal your woundedness.

GETTING REAL ABOUT THE PROBLEMS

Obviously I made a major mistake in allowing my online contact with this person to become too intimate. But to really understand how I got to this place, I had to dig a lot deeper. What was it about my situation that made me vulnerable to something like this? What precautions could I have taken to prevent this from happening, or to keep it from progressing as far as it did? What did I do wrong that set the stage for my downfall?

1. I tried to solve my emotional issues with spiritual formation.

I was seeking God. I was praying. I was working through Bible studies. I was memorizing Scripture. I was fasting. I was doing everything I knew how to do to grow closer to God. But these activities didn't address my emotional issues. Spiritual disciplines alone cannot solve emotional brokenness! That simply won't work. It's like trying to heal a broken leg with nothing but antibiotics.

I wasn't living out of my true emotions. I had unhealthy emoting and relating patterns. I was spending so much time trying to please so many people that I had no idea who I was. I had suppressed my emotional needs for so long for the sake of pressing on with ministry I no longer had a clue what I needed or that my needs were going unmet.

Ministry propagates the lie that you need to deny your emotional needs and care for everyone else. Ministry encourages autonomy in ministry marriages—dividing to conquer is seen as laudable. Congregants may give lip service to desiring authenticity from their leaders/pastors, but in truth are terrified of our being real and often recoil from our flaws.

If you're just beginning a career in ministry, go get counseling! If you have emotional issues (and we all do), get counseling! If you're married and in ministry, get counseling! If you're leaving one ministry position and moving into a new one, get counseling! In short, if you're in ministry, *get counseling*!

When I went into my first counseling session, I thought I knew what all my issues were and what I needed to pray about to fix them. I was so off base. I needed the support and wisdom of a professional counselor to even begin to see what the real issues were. Although I knew and could teach all the right answers, I was living out of faulty theology of perfection. Ministry is hard. We need one another, and we need a place where we can be completely transparent and real without immediate consequences. For most of us that place is only found in the safety of a counseling relationship.

2. Accountability partners weren't enough.
I had multiple accountability partners, but they didn't even see my emotional neediness. If you're emotionally aloof like I am, you probably don't even acknowledge your emotional issues; in fact, you might not even be aware of them. I was living off my spiritual life while my emotions were screaming out in agony. Given the wrong circumstances, sin can happen to anyone.

In my case, I was emotionally starved. I'd never learned how to value or care for my emotional needs. And those emotions were winning the battle for my soul. I fell time and time again over a period of months.

3. I didn't have true community surrounding me.

I believe ministry can set us up for emotional illness. We think being a spiritual leader means being autonomous and stoic and never losing our tempers. In an attempt to be spiritual, we push our "negative" emotions back inside.

Often we think we know what's wrong with us only to later learn the thing we'd thought was the big problem really wasn't the issue at all. It takes confessing your sins aloud to another person, as well as some really good counseling or spiritual direction, to discover your deep woundedness. And the fact of the matter is, if you're in ministry, *you're wounded!*

In ministry circles we give great lip service to the damage ministry can do to our marriages. I've been a part of many, many conversations with both pastors and their spouses, and I'm convinced people in ministry *know* what the pressure and demands of ministry can do to relationships. So why in the heck do we react so badly, so judgmentally, with so little compassion, when someone falls?

> I'M CONVINCED PEOPLE IN MINISTRY KNOW WHAT THE PRESSURE AND DEMANDS OF MINISTRY CAN DO TO RELATIONSHIPS. SO WHY IN THE HECK DO WE REACT SO BADLY, SO JUDGMENTALLY, WITH SO LITTLE COMPASSION, WHEN SOMEONE FALLS?

It's as if we believe if you do everything right and try to obey all the rules, you'll never fall—and you'll certainly never fall if you're a minister. But if spiritual warfare is a reality (and we know it is), there will be people who are wounded. There will be casualties. Why do we not have spiritual medevac teams and an emotional Red Cross to deal with the realities of the war zone in which we live and work?

4. I lacked the tools to deal with negative emotions.

I grew up in a home that didn't allow negative emotions. My biological mother died when I was 12. When my dad told me about her death, he ended by saying, "Praise the Lord, anyway." The grieving process was not honored or valued in our home.

I married a pastor when I was 20 and overnight went from being an undergrad at Asbury College to being the wife of a senior pastor of a congregation of 400 families in Belfast, Northern Ireland. I quickly learned the pastorate didn't favor negative emotions either, and many painful lessons reinforced my unhealthy pattern of burying emotions or becoming aloof to them. When I experienced negative emotions, I pushed them aside in the name of spiritual maturity. But you can't choose which emotions you will or won't feel. If you bury one you tend to bury them all. If you bury your emotions, they will manifest themselves in unhealthy ways.

> YOU CAN'T CHOOSE WHICH EMOTIONS YOU WILL OR WON'T FEEL. IF YOU BURY ONE YOU TEND TO BURY THEM ALL. IF YOU BURY YOUR EMOTIONS, THEY WILL MANIFEST THEMSELVES IN UNHEALTHY WAYS.

In his book *Love Busters*, Willard F. Harley lists "angry outbursts" as the number one "love buster." My husband is a very passionate and gifted prophet—but he will be the first to admit, even from the pulpit, that he has anger issues. For years he has said, "I only have one emotion—anger." Coming into our marriage, I didn't deal well with or have the tools for dealing with negative emotions. This caused me to become even more aloof from my husband. I began to see the church as my husband's mistress and co-workers as the embodiment of that mistress. I felt cheated, and feelings of entitlement grew in my heart.

5. My theology was very legalistic and inflexible.

I *was* very legalistic. I lived by rules. (I am, at heart, a Methodist.) Not only was I living out of a theology of perfection rather than one of grace, but my faith was also very linear. I believed that if you did A and then B and then C, you would always end up with D. I was disillusioned with my results. But rather than seeing the formula as the culprit, I began to blame God. I felt I'd followed the rules, yet he was holding out on me. In truth it was the rules and legalism that failed me. I vowed never to go online again, but I did. We created boundaries and I didn't IM for a while. But in the end I was emotionally unhealthy and emotionally dependent, and I fell back into it.

I've also learned the core sin I deal with is pride—but not in the way that word is most often understood. I struggle with the kind of pride that Don Richard Riso describes in *Personality Types*: "Pride refers to an inability or unwillingness to acknowledge one's own suffering; to deny many of their own needs while attempting to 'help' others. This passion could also be described as vainglory—pride in one's own virtue."

Man, that played right into my holiness upbringing. We sanctified folks do not sin, you know? And that belief about our own virtue is what can make it so hard for us to accept when we do fail.

FINDING HOPE

In the midst of my darkest nights, I cried out to God. And, I dare say, he heard my cry. Some of the most intimate moments with my Savior were in the midst of this valley experience. I wrote this piece from the abbey where I go for solitude:

> I am sitting on a wooden slat bench under the most amazing tree at the foot of the abbey. It is cool and the wind is blowing, reminding me of your touch, oh God—your presence. The bells have just chimed the hour, and the monks have begun singing. When I breathe in, it is like breathing in your very breath—your presence surrounds me so that I can taste it. You are so very tangible to me. I want to remember every nuance to treasure this moment in the depth of my being. At this moment I KNOW and FEEL that I am my Beloved's and you are mine. This birch tree is so full, so covered with Spanish moss that there are barely any leaves left. It is magical, mystical, like the beard of God. You know me so well, so intimately, that you are able to speak to all my senses.
>
> The assigned reading today grabbed my heart; you have spoken so clearly to me. Mark 10:17-22, especially verse 21: "And Jesus looked at him and LOVED him."
>
> My precious Lord, I think I have it bad, connecting with people and getting attached so quickly. You understand. You feel it too, only so much more deeply and with SO many people. So many who

touched your life and needed your touch. You wanted to win them, wanted their love, and DESERVED their love…

Wow… How many did you "look at" and "love" only to see them walk away?

Oh, and I am SUCH a SILLY girl, thinking I have a clue how to love or a CLUE about heartache and longing.

Sweet Jesus, I want so desperately to love you like that—DEEP-LY, MADLY, SOLELY. For you to be my ALL in ALL!

When you find yourself at the point of crisis, you're forced to deal with your "stuff." It may seem like hell, but it's actually a gift. Those difficult times when you must admit your own weakness and your total reliance on God leave you uniquely poised to take drastic measures. Take full advantage of that. You'll make greater strides in the darkest of nights than you can imagine. There will be days where all you can do is recite, "The Lord is my Shepherd" over and over again—but one day you will wake up and be whole. God is your Redeemer! There is *nothing* he cannot or will not redeem!

I experienced quite a few long and intense counseling sessions where my heart was ripped open and exposed for all of its fallenness, and my errant theology was revealed. I was usually quite stoic in the sessions—but it would often really hit me during my 90-minute drive home. Alone and unseen in the car, I wept. And then I would call Denny and relate the painful revelations of the last 90 minutes.

I still believe all ministers should be in counseling—not just in times when we find ourselves in crisis, but continually. At some point my own counseling shifted and became more spiritual direction, but I still go. I have two counselors available to give me their time. Elton, the counselor my credentials committee mandated for me, is still a resource for me, but he's far away, so I now see another counselor, Michele, who's only 10 minutes away. Sometimes she and I have formal counseling sessions, and other times we just go get coffee—but she is a permanent fixture in my life.

When we're able to admit our own need, we make it possible for others to be vehicles of God's grace to us. The restoration advisor from the credentials committee was such a grace in the midst of these tough days. One day I dragged into his office, all defeated after one of these marathon counseling sessions with Elton, and said, "How the heck did I even cook dinner? I am so messed up!"

He laughed and said, "Mary, I feel the same way! In my small group this week, our counselor had each of us do a genogram, which is like a family tree, except you have to indicate the emotional relationships between the family members and highlight all the broken relationships. I'm messed up! In fact I think the only two people in the room who had genograms worse than mine were the leaders!"

> WHEN WE'RE ABLE TO ADMIT OUR OWN NEED, WE MAKE IT POSSIBLE FOR OTHERS TO BE VEHICLES OF GOD'S GRACE TO US.

As I related my story to others and listened to others tell their own stories, I began to see I'm not so unique. I'm not alone—and neither are you. We've all been shaped by our families in good and bad ways. We've all been severely affected by our roles in ministry and the expectations placed on us. God did not, does not, and will not reject me in the midst of my brokenness. He did not kick me out of the park. He walked beside me in the valley of the shadow of death and he brought me through. He knows how I'm formed and remembers I'm dust and yet, his love abounds for me.

CHAPTER 15

WHEN A FUN TRIP FALLS APART

By Matthew McNutt

I WAS SITTING IN THE FRONT SEAT OF THE PARKED CAR, completely drenched and staring out the window as the rain poured relentlessly. After looking forward to this trip for months, I was overwhelmed by the degree to which everything had gone wrong. I looked to the left and right of me and saw the same scene—other frustrated, tired, and overwhelmed youth leaders sitting in cars loaded with soaking wet teenagers. The only difference was those other leaders were all looking to me for an answer.

> AFTER LOOKING FORWARD TO THIS TRIP FOR MONTHS, I WAS OVERWHELMED BY THE DEGREE TO WHICH EVERYTHING HAD GONE WRONG.

And I didn't have one.

I was serving in my first full-time youth ministry position. I'd started there a couple of years earlier, fresh out of college, with lots of enthusiasm, but not much experience. The church was in Connecticut, just a few hours' drive from a huge New Jersey theme park, complete with roller coasters, stage shows, and even a large drive-through safari. (Any time you can plan a trip in which a monkey poops on your car, you know it's a youth ministry winner!) Plus the park has a Christian music festival each year, so it seemed perfect for us. Each year we would load up the vehicles, set up camp at a local state park, and hit the rides from sunup to sundown. While snow camps and concerts attracted more kids, this annual summer trip was perhaps our most talked-about event—probably because it was my favorite, and I looked forward to it all year!

During my first two years the trips were beyond my expectations. But then came year 3. As the trip approached, I felt a little nervous. Only one or two of the 20 kids signed up for the trip were "regulars," and the majority of the group hadn't really been involved in our youth ministry before. I was a little worried these kids might not have fun since they didn't know each other well. But I figured my leaders and I could work overtime to build connections, and ultimately, the trip would be a great success if it enabled us to build relationships with some new kids.

Our first day in the park was awesome. The rides were amazing, the lines were short, and we were having a blast. The Newsboys played in concert that night and they rocked the crowd hard. But after the last encore, when the lights came on and the park began to close down for the night, it quickly became apparent something was wrong: Two of our kids were missing—including one whose mom was chaperoning the trip. It didn't take long for that mom to begin panicking.

For the next two hours we searched the park, trying to get security to help us. (They don't get involved unless somebody is missing significantly longer.) We retraced our steps over and over but came up with nothing. We could hear security radios buzzing about some kind of violence in the now-closed park and police were rushing onto the scene. It didn't look good.

I was starting to fear the worst when the two kids suddenly appeared! They'd managed to get backstage to meet the Newsboys, and that's where they'd been the whole time! I wanted to throttle them (I did restrain myself, as the mom was right there), but at the same time I had to be honest with myself: Kids are going to be kids, and the Newsboys are cool. I was the paid youth pastor, but I might have been tempted to blow off the group for a few hours if I'd had a chance to meet the band.

Finally we were able to leave the park and head back to camp. I was physically and emotionally drained, as were the rest of my leaders. I was eager for the day to be over, but before bed, I still had to talk consequences with my stage crashers and calm down some of my more frazzled leaders. By the time my head hit my pillow, it was well after midnight and I instantly fell asleep.

Morning came way too soon. As I began to wake, my mind moving in slow motion, my surroundings grew clearer. I'm camping. It's a youth group trip. I'm freezing. It's day 2. I've wet my sleeping bag. We had a scare last night, but hopefully everyone has calmed down. Wait: *I wet my sleeping bag?* I'm a grown man in a tent full of teenage guys—this can't be happening! The shock got my adrenaline going and the world suddenly snapped into focus.

The good news was that I hadn't actually wet my sleeping bag. But it was definitely wet—soaked, in fact. I was lying in two inches of water, which explained why I was so chilled. I reached over to my duffel bag to grab some dry clothes and was horrified to find that water had soaked up through my bag during the night. Everything was wet. As I listened to the sound of rain pounding on the tent, I began to realize my favorite trip had taken another turn for the worse.

Meanwhile the other guys in the tent were beginning to wake up. Their moans and yelps confirmed they were in the same position as me—soaked with nothing dry to change into. I could hear confused and upset voices outside the tent, so I climbed out to see what was happening. Our tent wasn't the only one—just about everyone had awakened in pools of rainwater. The fierce wind from the storm had blown the rain guards off our tents, and the downpour did the rest. Kids and adults all scrambled to the vehicles to get out of the wet weather.

And that's how I found myself sitting in the driver's seat of my car, soaked to the bone, watching my favorite event fall to pieces around me. I was completely and totally overwhelmed. Kids going missing in the park. leaders losing it, and now this? I had no idea what to do, but I didn't want to admit that to the shell-shocked teens huddled in the car with me. As the storm raged outside, another battle raged inside my mind. I knew the trip was a bust. There wasn't a laundromat big enough to handle all our clothes, sleeping bags, and other gear. And even if we could get all that stuff dry, what about the tents? There was no way to dry them out in this weather! Obviously, we couldn't camp out for another night with nothing dry to change into. I didn't want to be the youth pastor who made the headlines by coming home with 20 teens stricken with pneumonia.

But here was my dilemma: I was terrified to cancel the event! I was afraid of what parents would say after paying so much on non-refundable tickets. What about the teens? Would I lose their respect for hyping an event that ended up falling apart? And honestly, I was afraid of my senior pastor's response as well. He had repeatedly driven home the principle that canceling meetings or events, or even scaling them back in any way, comes across as failure—and that is not an option. Everything had to be growing, always getting bigger and better; otherwise the leadership was weak and people would go somewhere else.

Finally, after 30 or 40 minutes of trying to come up with some way to salvage the trip and avoid coming home with my tail tucked between my legs, I acknowledged the truth. For the safety of the kids entrusted to my care and responsibility, we had to leave. I broke the news to the adults and students, who actually seemed relieved to hear it. As the rain continued to pour, we quickly took down the tents, packed the bags, grabbed our garbage, and loaded the vehicles. I hadn't thought we could get any more soaked, but wow, I was wrong!

Since we hadn't even been able to eat because of the weather, our first stop was to grab breakfast at a fast-food place. And then we hit the road toward home. The plan was pretty simple—we'd book it back to Connecticut and any kids who wanted to could spend the night at my tiny house. We'd take turns running their sleeping bags and wet clothes through the dryer while we stayed up watching movies, eating pizza, and playing card games. Or if they preferred, they could just head home. It was the only thing I could come up with to try to salvage the weekend.

Most of the teens opted to spend the night at my place, and a couple of our adults made the plunge as well. And I was shocked by just how much fun we had that night! In my mind, a wet night at my house wasn't much compared with a day at the theme park, but we had a blast! Maybe it was the feeling of having survived a horrific ordeal that bonded us all together, but we spent the night laughing, joking, and horsing around, and ultimately forged some incredible relationships with kids I'd hardly even known just 48 hours earlier.

Years later that event is still the most talked-about and fondly remembered trip of my whole time at that church! Other teens were actually jealous they missed out on the adventure! The event I'd been afraid would become my undoing as a youth pastor actually became one of the best community builders I've ever experienced anywhere. Who would have imagined that canceling the year's most popular event could actually strengthen the ministry?

WEATHERING THE STORM

My story has a happy ending, but that doesn't mean I didn't make a few critical mistakes. The whole thing could have been much less painful and terrifying for me if I'd done a few things differently. Looking back, here's what I did wrong:

1. I was more concerned about the reactions of the parents and my senior pastor than the safety of the kids.

When I'm really honest with myself, that's one of the truths I have to face. If I hadn't been so afraid of how parents and my pastor might react, I wouldn't have spent half an hour agonizing over what to do. I would have known I needed to get that group of soaking, freezing teens home and dry ASAP. I let my fear of their reactions and the appearance of failure immobilize me.

2. I didn't have a backup plan!

I hadn't thought through how I'd handle kids getting lost, bad weather, catastrophic tent failure, or bear attacks! (Okay, that last one didn't happen, but remember—there were monkeys pooping on the cars. Crazy stuff happens when you're traveling with a bunch of teens!) I didn't have any kind of plan for what I'd do if things went bad. What if a vehicle died? What if a tent broke? What if weather shut down the park? What if? It had not occurred to me that anything could go wrong.

Since I'd already done this event successfully a couple of times, I think I got comfortable—which is my nice way of saying I got lazy. Yes, I had everything I needed to camp and hit the theme park, but that's all. I wasn't prepared for anything to go wrong or even vary from previous years. I should have mapped out a backup plan and exit strategy if something were to go wrong. I should have thought about how I'd handle it if we needed to cancel for whatever reason.

Having such plans in place is important—regardless of the size of the event. For smaller events, such preparation might mean having a rain date, an alternate plan, and a clear understanding about conditions that would warrant the event being canceled. For a larger event or trip it might also include communicating about what circumstances would require certain individuals or the entire group heading home and how that would be done. This way people aren't caught off guard when an unfortunate situation arises—they've already thought about those conditions and how they'll respond. That preparation would also include communicating the basics of the plans to parents, leaders, and other church leaders. If I'd informed parents and my senior pastor about what I'd do if we were forced to cut the trip short, I'd have been much less stressed about their potential reactions.

3. I handled the missing teens situation poorly.

I wasn't very successful in handling the episode with the missing kids—unless my goal was to ramp the tension level way up! When we realized the kids were missing, I kept everyone at the park, even though the camp was only a few miles away. I didn't want to send the other youth out searching late at night—so pretty much all they were doing was speculating about how bad it might be, adding stress to the panicked mother. I should have sent the majority of the group back to the campsite while a couple of other adults remained with me to search for the two missing kids.

Any time a student goes missing it is stressful; if there's any way to remove distractions, do so. It would've been better for the rest of the youth to be at the tents resting instead of watching a panicked mother become (legitimately) more and more frightened. Now that I have children of my own and know the terror of their wandering out of my sight in a public place for even just a few moments, I'm embarrassed at my lack of understanding for this mother who didn't know where her daughter was for two hours. I should have been much more focused on her and let my other leaders take care of the group.

4. I was more focused on the event's activity than the event's purpose.
Somewhere along the way I came to believe giving kids a fun time at the theme park was the whole point of the event. But the reality is that the rides, the concert, and camping were all just means to an end. The purpose of the trip was to make and strengthen connections and relationships between adult leaders and students. But because I lost track of that, I put too much energy into salvaging a trip to a theme park instead of brainstorming alternate ways to achieve the actual purpose.

> BY CLEARLY DEFINING THE PURPOSE OF AN ACTIVITY, WE LEAVE MORE ROOM FOR FLEXIBILITY.

I should've had a clearly defined purpose statement for the event—a statement I'd communicated to my adult leaders and reminded myself of repeatedly. Ideally I'd have provided every leader with a typed-up trip agenda with emergency phone numbers and other details, and I'd have put the purpose statement in bold letters across the top. When I woke up soaking wet, if I'd remembered the goal of the trip was to build relationships between adult leaders and students, I'd have been quicker to realize we could still fulfill that purpose with a sleepover back at my house. By clearly defining the purpose of an activity, we leave more room for flexibility. We can make changes more easily, responding to situational issues and environmental factors as needed, because the critical issue isn't making sure the specific activity happens as we'd planned. Often the purpose can be fulfilled in other ways.

FINDING HOPE

In hindsight I can't believe I was so terrified of canceling the remainder of the trip we'd planned. I was so wrapped up in my definition of success and the appearance of having a perfect youth program that I thought any hint of pulling back would come across as failure and inability to lead. In reality, parents appreciate a youth worker who values the safety of their children enough to make the sometimes tough and unpopular call to cancel or redirect an event. Whether it's because too many chaperones backed out at the last minute, weather is making the activity dangerous, or some other scenario has arisen that puts your students at risk, canceling because of safety issues demonstrates your priorities are on track and you're worthy of the incredible trust parents grant in allowing their children to be under your care.

And here's the most remarkable thing for me: This event that seemed so horrific at the time—this trip I feared would end my career at that church and forever destroy my popularity with students—represents one of my favorite memories from my time with that congregation. By redirecting the event to our home, we salvaged the weekend and stayed on track with the ultimate purpose of the event. It's remarkable how God can take something we think is a lost cause and transform it into something of great value for the kingdom! Instead of losing all these new students who signed up for the first time, we gained a number of regular participants! And several of those students went on to become spiritual leaders in the group in the years that followed.

If you're struggling with a decision about canceling an event, know that God will honor your courage in doing the more difficult thing. And as big as it may seem in the moment, when the dust has settled and you've had the benefit of some time and rest, you'll most likely find it was not nearly as bad as you'd feared. We tend to imagine the worst-case scenario, but our worst fears almost never come to pass. Our God is a powerful God—one who's able to bring beauty out of the ashes of your canceled event.

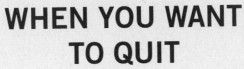

CHAPTER 16

WHEN YOU WANT TO QUIT

By Ginny Olson

IT WAS A GORGEOUS SUMMER EVENING. THE WARM, VELVET breeze and pink sky were enticing people to abandon their air-conditioned cars and get outside. I decided to walk to church for Wednesday night Bible study—partly so I could bask in the rare evening, but mostly because I was procrastinating. Walking meant I could literally drag my heels on my way to church. Heading to youth group that night felt like an act of weary obedience. It wasn't just a habit at this point; it was a rut. And if I were to be completely honest, even though I might have dreamed of other options, physically I had no energy left to choose to do anything else.

As I plodded along, I began to daydream about escaping to another life. It occurred to me that if I kept walking past the church, I could stop by an ATM and empty my account. Then I could continue on to the airport and catch a plane to China. (That wasn't as random as it might sound. I had a friend who was teaching English in China at that time, so I figured at least I'd have a place to stay.)

It was my third year in ministry, and it was obvious I'd already passed the stage of exhaustion. Students would choke up describing the conflicts they were having. I'd nod my head in an attempt to portray empathetic listening the way I'd learned in youth worker seminars. But if those kids could've seen beneath the skin, they'd have seen a heart of stone. Volunteers would come with a question about a small-group event they were planning, and I'd look at them blankly and shrug my shoulders. *Figure it out yourself* is what I was thinking. I felt nothing.

I was in the stage of, "I don't give a @%$#%@. And I don't give a @%$#%@ if it bothers you that I used the word @%$#%@."

A pretty desperate state for a Baptist girl.

I've since learned that I was in burnout. Not the lightweight "burned out" we talk about when we're bone tired after leading an all-night outreach event. This was the full-blown, beyond fatigued, emotionally numb, dangerous state of burnout that's often a by-product of being in a people-helping profession.

How on Earth had I gotten to this point? I'd started in youth ministry right out of college, fresh with a degree in biblical and theological studies. I grew up in a generation that believed we really could change the world. I'd joined a team of passionate youth workers at a megachurch who took that charge seriously. We were a formidable force, trusting God would do miracles in our city through us. We had dreams of filling the city's professional sports arena with students who would hear about the love and salvation of God. We were constantly teaching, preaching, studying Scripture, counseling, sharing our faith, and leading mission trips, service projects, vacation Bible school, camps, and retreats. We were hanging out at local schools, speaking in classes, coaching sports, and going to every imaginable school play, concert, or competition.

We were also spending time in community where we'd talk about how busy our schedules were and how we needed to change and get time alone with God. We swore we'd hold each other accountable, but that accountability seemed to be just one more thing on our "to do" lists. To our credit, we also laughed hard, played hard, and prayed hard together. But we didn't realize that many of us were also living hard; not in the country music clichéd way, but in a way that didn't allow for space for a life outside of the ministry. It was a lifestyle that was costing me my soul.

If this weren't enough, the head of our ministry had resigned a few months before. John left big shoes to fill. He was a charismatic, experienced, and visionary leader who enthralled the junior highers with his stories. When John would teach, God seemed to move and kids' lives were changed. The youth group became the place to be for kids in the community. Parents loved the way their seventh-, eighth-, and ninth-graders were excited to come to church and would load up their minivans with their kids' friends. We had times of prayer where, instead of asking for God's help for their grandmother's ingrown toenails, adolescents were spending 30 minutes or more pleading for their friends and family members with a gut-wrenching rawness that debunked any myth that kids that age couldn't have a deep faith.

We were in Camelot and we knew it. That is, until the day John informed the team God was leading him elsewhere—and with that, Camelot evaporated. As the veteran staff member at age 23, I was designated as the interim leader of the junior high ministry. Even though my teammates assured me that no one expected the ministry to continue on the same track it had been on, I knew the external expectations were high. My internal ones were even higher. And I was terrified.

> I LOOKED AT MY SCHEDULE AND REALIZED I'D BEEN HOME ONLY SIX NIGHTS IN THE PAST YEAR—AND THAT INCLUDED CHRISTMAS, EASTER, AND THANKSGIVING.

As I stated earlier, we'd been working hard even before he left. After my desolate walk to church that summer evening, I looked at my schedule and realized I'd been home only six nights in the past year—and that included Christmas, Easter, and Thanksgiving. One would think this realization would've slowed me down. But I wore the overwork as a badge of honor. In my burned-out stage, I had become a martyr. No one worked as hard as I worked. I might not be as charismatic as my predecessor, but I would outwork him. Or, to be more precise, I was trying to outwork the legend of him.

Despite how drained I was that summer, we still had to get ready for camp. Our ministry ran its own weeklong camp session at the end of every summer. One hundred fifty kids. Twenty leaders. It was the highlight of the year. We went from early morning until late at night. Our philosophy was that tired kids didn't get into trouble. No one questioned the price staff members were paying for that philosophy, at least not out loud. "Sacrifice for the cause" was our attitude. The adage "It's better to burn out than rust out" was my mantra. It never occurred to me that, either way, you're out.

We were about four days into the camp and kids were running around playing one last game of "capture the flag" before evening chapel. The sun hung low in the sky as I sat on the chapel steps and looked around the campgrounds. In this rare quiet moment, I reflected on the state I was in. *Do I really want to keep doing this?* I was tired of the schedule, the demands, and the quest to live up to expectations. I was ready to quit—not just quit this job, but quit ministry altogether. Yet somewhere deep inside, there was a part of me still desperately striving for validation. That became clear as I ventured to query God. "Are you pleased?" I asked. "Are you pleased with what you're seeing?" I paused before I sheepishly asked the next question: "Am I doing a good job?"

I'll never forget God's response. It was one of the few times in my life when I knew without a doubt that God was communicating with me. I sensed strongly his firm, quiet voice saying, "Ginny, I love you. This camp could be the worst experience ever for the students and the leaders and I will love you anyway. I don't love you because of what you do for me. I love you because I love you."

And in that moment, I felt a crack in my burned-out numbness. I had a sense of hope as I grappled with this new perspective. God's love wasn't dependent on my performance? Of course, I had memorized Ephesians 2:8-9: "For it is by grace you have been saved, through faith—and this is not from yourselves, it is the gift of God—not by works, so that no one can boast." But in that moment, I got a new and deepened sense of how that truth applied to my own work in ministry.

I'd love to say that from that moment I continually walked in that new state of grace, but the reality is that I fell back into old habits a lot—and I still do from time to time. It took several years for me to really comprehend that ministry needs to flow at God's pace, not mine.

Eventually, I did resign. But I quit that job, not ministry. And I made sure the next position I took was one that would allow me to maintain a healthy pace of life.

SIGNS ON THE ROAD TO BURNOUT

As I've analyzed that season of my life and ministry, I've come to realize there were several factors that led to my experience of burnout:

1. I had an unclear and inadequate understanding of grace.

I was raised in a culture that elevated performance. Those who worked hard and did well were given praise and attention. When it came to my faith, I transferred those same values to my relationship with God. I believed that the harder I worked, the more value I would be to the kingdom, and the more God would value me. My Christianity had become more influenced by cultural and individual expectations than by Scripture and a solid identity grounded in Christ.

> I BELIEVED THAT THE HARDER I WORKED, THE MORE VALUE I WOULD BE TO THE KINGDOM, AND THE MORE GOD WOULD VALUE ME. MY CHRISTIANITY HAD BECOME MORE INFLUENCED BY CULTURAL AND INDIVIDUAL EXPECTATIONS THAN BY SCRIPTURE AND A SOLID IDENTITY GROUNDED IN CHRIST.

2. I failed to honor the Sabbath.

Because I was working in church ministry, I knew Sundays weren't the time when I could rest and recharge my batteries. I had far too many responsibilities on Sundays for those days to be true Sabbath for me. So I would attempt to take Fridays off. But there always seemed to be a student's game to go to or a concert to attend on Friday evening. The result was that I never took a full day off. There were people who confronted me on that—but in my burned-out state, I arrogantly believed I knew what was best.

3. I wasn't willing to look at the issues driving me.

One of the many reasons I kept going at such an unforgiving pace was that it meant I didn't have to stop and do the hard work of reflection. Truth be told, it was painful to face my insecurities and inadequacies. Staying busy meant I didn't have to feel the pain.

HOPE-FILLED TRANSFORMATION

Since that season of burnout, I've made some changes to help maintain a healthier pace in life and ministry. Although I'm still in process, I have found these practices and values have kept me from reentering that phase.

One important change was seeking out people who could help me dig into the underlying issues. I often tell youth workers to find three people when they move to a new community: A reliable mechanic, a knowledgeable doctor, and a good therapist or spiritual director. In the years since my own experience of burnout, I've seen both a therapist and a spiritual director. Both of these individuals and their differing approaches have been valuable in helping to delve beneath the mask and help understand some of the forces that drive me. They've also offered ongoing help and support as I sought to make changes in my lifestyle.

> I OFTEN TELL YOUTH WORKERS TO FIND THREE PEOPLE WHEN THEY MOVE TO A NEW COMMUNITY: A RELIABLE MECHANIC, A KNOWLEDGEABLE DOCTOR, AND A GOOD THERAPIST OR SPIRITUAL DIRECTOR.

Another hope-restoring adjustment was making a real commitment to keeping a weekly Sabbath. Once I began to practice a weekly Sabbath, I noticed a difference in how I responded to life. I wasn't as crabby or short-tempered when unexpected interruptions occurred. I found I didn't respond with "tired" anytime someone asked how I was feeling. Instead, my response was more frequently "great" or "excited" or "loving life." I also noticed a rise in my creative juices after years of dormancy. I even began to take classes in sculpting and drawing.

I've also recognized the importance of investing in relationships that have nothing to do with my job. When I first reflected on what my life would look like if I quit my ministry position, I realized I had very few friends who weren't connected to my job in one way or another. In my quest to be focused and "change the world," I'd neglected any friends who weren't in that circle. One step toward my becoming healthy was to begin to invest more in my friendships with people who were unconnected with ministry. I quickly discovered my life was richer because of these relationships. These friends were able to offer a perspective on life that I wasn't able to access when I was immersed in my little world. And I found myself tracking with their healthier pace of life.

A final change I made was deciding to pursue further education that would strengthen my ministry skills. I realized that even though I was working hard, I wasn't always working smart. I knew *how* things worked in youth ministry, but I wasn't always clear on *why*. In fact, taking a break from ministry so I could attend graduate school is part of what allowed me to continue in youth ministry rather than leaving the field altogether. In grad school I was challenged to evaluate my experience against Scripture, differing theories of ministry, and the wisdom of those who had gone before me. My course of study helped me understand why my own inadequate theology and philosophy of ministry had gotten me to the point of burnout. I was able to reflect, retool, and eventually, reenter the world of ministry.

I was cautious when I made my return to youth ministry, doing all I could to make sure I found a place where I could maintain a lifestyle that was emotionally healthy and spiritually life-giving. I ended up serving with a team of colleagues who actually took two days off in a row, who understood they weren't the saviors of the junior highers in our area, who had lives outside of our ministry, and who valued counseling. I was amazed to see volunteers who'd served in that ministry for more than 10 years and were still going strong. As a team we had seasons where we worked very hard, but we also had seasons of rest when the ministry pace would slow down. We practically shut down for a month every summer. And the amazing thing was that God was still present. Kids still came to Christ. And in the midst of it, I sensed God's pleasure.

CONTRIBUTORS

Dave Ambrose ("When the Van Breaks Down") has been working with students and adult youth workers for 17 years. He is currently overseeing the youth ministry at BridgeWay Community Church near Indianapolis, Indiana. Dave is a trainer for Youth Specialties and speaks frequently at retreats and youth worker training events all over the world. Dave's first book, *Chew on This*, a collection of guided spiritual meditations for students, was published by Zondervan in 2008. Dave's favorite thing to do in the entire world is dancing with his two boys, Josh and Ty, and their dog, Raider, in the living room. Dave's wife, Melody, usually just sits back and laughs at them all! Check out more about Dave at www.daveambrose.tv or www.daveambrose.blogspot.com.

Tim Baker ("When You Lose Your Cool with a Parent") is the author of numerous books, including *Broken, The Way I See It*, and the award-winning *Extreme Faith*. He's the managing editor of *The Journal of Student Ministries* and a regular columnist for *Youthwalk* magazine. Tim is the director of student ministries at Hope Fellowship and lives in Longview, Texas, with his wife, Jacqui, and their three kids. Find out more about Tim at www.timbaker.cc.

Pete Brokopp ("When Tragedy Strikes Your Ministry") has been a missionary with the Christian and Missionary Alliance in Burkina Faso, West Africa, for more than 10 years. Pete grew up in Gabon, Africa, where his parents were missionaries. From 1993 to 1998 he was a youth pastor of First Alliance Church in Lexington, North Carolina. In the midst of a successful and enjoyable youth ministry, he experienced God's call to West Africa to work with youth there. He studied French in Burkina Faso, where he met his wife, Alice. They were married in 2000. In addition to establishing disciple-making youth ministries in 800 churches in southwest Burkina Faso, being involved in the local church, and raising two children, Charity Grace and Samuel Peter, they also host teams and are involved in many building projects.

Rick Bundschuh ("When Your Office Is a Wreck") is a pastor, veteran youth worker, writer, speaker, and cartoonist based in Kauai, Hawaii. Rick is known for his creativity, over-the-top imagination, and successful efforts in reaching unchurched teens. In 1991 Rick (along a with a few other "mad hatters") founded Kauai Christian Fellowship, a church that has earned its reputation for being high-energy, amplified, and postmodern oriented. Rick serves as a teaching pastor at Kauai Christian Fellowship and continues to write and illustrate material for various publishers. He lives in Poipu, Hawaii, with his beautiful wife, Lauren, their kids, a weenie dog, and a quiver of surfboards.

Len Evans ("When You're Fired") has been a youth pastor (and between churches, a waiter, warehouse worker, telemarketer, and jackhammer operator) since graduating from Dallas Theological Seminary in 1994. He's the author of *Creative Bible Lessons on 1 and 2 Timothy and Titus* and has written for many youth ministry magazines. He's blessed to be the youth pastor of Melonie Park Church in Lubbock, Texas, where he occasionally still gets giddy when he goes to work. He's more blessed by being married to Tonja and being the father of Taylor and Sara Beth.

Mary Huebner ("When You Fail Morally") has been involved in youth ministry for nearly three decades, serving in Northern Ireland, Wisconsin, Ohio, and now in Florida. She and her husband, Sr. Pastor Dennis Huebner, have three sons, two of whom are also involved in youth ministry. Mary currently leads the middle school girls small group at Oak Grove Church of God in Tampa, Florida. Mary is the author of *Deal with It* (Zondervan, 2009). She has been a professional curriculum writer for the last 10 years as well as a contributing writer for several youth ministry magazines.

Dale Kaufman ("When Your Spouse Feels Ignored") is an ordained minister in the Free Methodist Church and has served in youth and family ministry for 28 years. He is married with two sons and currently serves as the senior pastor of the Free Methodist Church in Monroe, Michigan. Through the years Dale has spoken at youth camps, marriage retreats, and family camps, and his articles have appeared in *Youthworker Journal* and *The Journal of Student Ministries*. He also serves on the board of directors for www.TheMarriageBed.com, an online ministry that seeks to build greater intimacy for married Christians.

Danette Matty ("When You Feel Worthless") has been a volunteer youth worker since big hair was in. She's also a wife and mom, freelance writer, speaker, and trainer with Group Publishing. She notes, "I changed the names of people in this article who were less than angelic because I'm a nice person. Liz is still serving God and angelic enough for me to use her real name."

Adam McLane ("When Crisis Rules the Ministry") is the online community manager for Youth Specialties, where he overseas the YS podcast and blog. After 10 years of professional work in local church youth ministry, he now happily volunteers at his local church. He and his family live in San Diego, California. You can connect with him at www.adammclane.com.

Matthew McNutt ("When a Fun Trip Falls Apart") is the associate pastor for student ministries at Brandywine Valley Baptist Church in Wilmington, Delaware. Matthew was a season 3 contestant on NBC's weight-loss reality show *The Biggest Loser*, on which he lost 176 pounds. He's a regular columnist for *The Journal of Student Ministries* and blogs regularly at www.matthewmcnutt.com.

Ginny Olson ("When You Want to Quit") is one of the directors of North Park University's Center for Youth Ministry Studies in Chicago, Illinois, where she works with both undergraduate and seminary students. She has been involved in youth ministry for more than 20 years at various churches and camps, including serving on staff in the junior high ministry at Willow Creek Community Church. She is the author of *Teenage Girls: Exploring Issues Adolescent Girls Face and Strategies to Help Them*, coauthor of *Youth Ministry Management Tools*, and was an editor and contributing writer for *Breaking the Gender Barrier in Youth Ministry*.

Will Penner ("When the Finances Fail") works four jobs to pay off his debt: He teaches English and journalism at East Hickman High School in Lyles, Tennessee; he's a consultant with Youth Ministry Architects; he's the resource director for YMToday.com; and he's the executive editor for *The Journal of Student Ministries*.

Dave Rahn ("When a Student Hates God") is the vice president and chief ministry officer for Youth for Christ USA and director of Huntington University's MA in Youth Ministry Leadership. He has been widely published in the areas of youth ministry theology, evangelism, and student leadership. Dave and Susie, his wife of 32 years, live in Indiana.

Jason Raitz ("When the Event Fails") is part of the Elevate staff team at Willow Creek Church near Chicago, where he works with an incredible group of people who make sure junior high kids are connected to caring adults and to one another. He has been a youth pastor since 1995 and loves to create environments for students to experience Jesus. When he's not dreaming up events for junior high kids, he tries to create awesome moments for his family. He and his wife, Tracie, have been married since 1997 and have four amazingly active and energy-filled kids. And he believes Ted Williams is the greatest hitter of all time.

Brenda Seefeldt ("When Parents Don't Respect You") has been doing youth ministry since 1981 and has served in her current church since 1990—the same year she began the youth ministry resource Wild Frontier (www.wildfrontier.org). Coincidence? No. She lives outside Washington, D.C.—the greatest city in the world—with her husband, John.

Ginger Sinsabaugh MacDonald ("When a Teen Gets Pregnant"), frustrated that the average dog food commercial was more memorable than the typical Sunday sermon, quit her full-time advertising gig to help youth leaders and outreach programs create a craving for Christ with the nonbeliever. She is the founder of TastyFaith resources for urban youth ministry, which you can find at www.TastyFaith.com.

Understanding God's will in their lives can be over-whelming for teens. We know that God is calling them to change the world, but how are they sup-posed to do that? This book helps students know that they were created for a purpose, defines for them how to discover God's call, and encourages them to use that to change the world.

Leave a Footprint Change the Whole World

Tim Baker
Retail $9.99
978-0-310-27885-6

Visit www.youthspecialties.com
or your local bookstore.